IV CONVENTIONS OF FORM AND APPEARANCE

27 Document Format *71*
a Clear and effective documents
b Academic papers
c Business correspondence

28 The Hyphen *85*
a Compound adjectives
b Fractions and compound numbers
c Prefixes and suffixes

29 Capital Letters *86*
a First word of sentence
b Proper nouns and adjectives
c Titles and subtitles of works
d Titles of persons

30 Underlining (Italics) *88*
a Titles of works
b Ships, aircraft, spacecraft, trains
c Foreign words
d Words, letters, and numbers named as words

31 Abbreviations *90*
a Titles before and after proper names
b Familiar abbreviations
c *BC, AD, AM, PM, no., $*
d Latin abbreviations
e Words usually spelled out (measurements, names, etc.)

32 Numbers *92*
a Numerals vs. words
b Commonly used numerals (days, years, etc.)
c Beginnings of sentences

V USING AND DOCUMENTING SOURCES

33 Evaluation and Synthesis of Sources *95*
a Evaluation
b Synthesis

34 Notes *96*
a Summary
b Paraphrase
c Direct quotation

35 Plagiarism *98*
a What not to acknowledge
b What to acknowledge
c How to avoid plagiarism

36 Introduction of Borrowed Material in Your Paper *101*

37 Documentation of Sources *103*

38 MLA Documentation Style *104*
a Parenthetical citations
b List of works cited

39 *Chicago Manual* Documentation Style *118*
a Endnotes or footnotes and works-cited entries
b Models

40 APA Documentation Style *125*
a Parenthetical citations
b Reference list

41 CBE Documentation Style *134*
a Numbered text citations
b Numbered references

Throughout the text, a small raised circle (°) follows every term defined in the Glossary of Terms (p. 151).

Glossary of Usage *139*
Glossary of Terms *151*
Index *165*

The
LITTLE, BROWN
ESSENTIAL HANDBOOK
for
WRITERS

Second Edition

Jane E. Aaron
New York University

 LONGMAN

An imprint of Addison Wesley Longman, Inc.

New York • Reading, Massachusetts • Menlo Park, California • Harlow, England
Don Mills, Ontario • Sydney • Mexico City • Madrid • Amsterdam

Senior Editor: Patricia Rossi
Developmental Editor: Thomas Maeglin
Project Editorial Manager: Robert Ginsberg
Design Manager: Sandra Watanabe
Text Designer: Dorothy Bungert/*EriBen Graphics*
Cover Designer: Kay Petronio
Art Studio: *EriBen Graphics*
Electronic Production Manager: Valerie A. Sawyer
Desktop Project Administrator: Jim Sullivan
Manufacturing Manager: Helene G. Landers
Electronic Page Makeup: Dorothy Bungert/*EriBen Graphics*
Printer and Binder: RR Donnelley and Sons Company
Cover Printer: The Lehigh Press, Inc.

Library of Congress Cataloging-in-Publication Data

Aaron, Jane E.
    The Little, Brown essential handbook for writers / Jane E.
  Aaron.—2nd ed.
        p.   cm.
  "Substantially abridges parts of The Little, Brown compact
handbook, by Jane E. Aaron, and The Little, Brown handbook,
by H. Ramsey Fowler and Jane E. Aaron"—T.p. verso.
  Includes index.
  ISBN 0-321-03805-3
  1. English language—Grammar—Handbooks, manuals,
etc.   2. English language—Rhetoric—Handbooks, manuals,
etc.   I. Title.
PE1112.A24   1996   96-8494
808'.042--dc20   CIP

Copyright © 1997 by Addison-Wesley Educational Publishers Inc.

The Little, Brown Essential Handbook for Writers substantially
abridges parts of *The Little, Brown Compact Handbook*, by Jane
E. Aaron, and *The Little, Brown Handbook*, by H. Ramsey Fowler
and Jane E. Aaron.

ISBN 0-321-03805-3

  2345678910—DOC—9998

USING THIS BOOK

This little book contains essential information for writers in and out of school. Clarity and style, grammar, punctuation, mechanics, source documentation, usage—all the basics appear in a convenient, accessible format. (To see how the book works, look at the visual guide inside the back cover.) Explanations consider writers who are unfamiliar with the terminology of writing: needless terms are omitted, and essential terms, marked °, are defined in the Glossary of Terms. Material especially for writers using English as a second language is marked ESL . Examples come from a wide range of subjects, science to literature to business.

This book aims to support you in documenting and editing your writing. Documenting sources helps make your writing informative and honest. Editing helps make it clear and effective—in other words, helps it *communicate*. For editing, you'll never need or use everything in this book because you already know much of what's here, whether consciously or not. The trick is to figure out what you *don't* know, focus on those areas, and back yourself up with this book. Discover what the book has to offer by scanning the Contents inside the front cover. Keep a list of mistakes and other writing problems that your readers point out to you. This list can be your personal editing checklist, setting your priorities. When using the checklist, don't try to find every mistake in a single reading: you may need to read once for repetition, say, and once for apostrophes. And read with your own eyes: don't depend too much on your computer's grammar or spelling checker because neither can catch every error (a spelling checker, for instance, can't distinguish between *no, not,* and *now*).

Editing your writing is important, but it occurs in a larger context. That's why the first thing you see inside the front cover is a Writer's Checklist covering the entire process of writing. Contrary to much popular opinion, writing is *not* solely, or even primarily, a matter of correctness. True, any written message will find a more receptive audience if it is correct in grammar, punctuation, and similar matters. But these should come late in the process, after you've allowed yourself to discover what you want to say and how you want to say it, freeing yourself to make mistakes along the way. As one writer put it, you need to get the clay on the potter's wheel before you can shape it into a bowl, and you need to shape the bowl before you can perfect it. So get your clay on the wheel and work with it until it looks like a bowl. Then consult this book.

Acknowledgments

Many teachers offered expert advice for this revision. Representing composition, literature, history, psychology, biology, business, and other disciplines, they are Douglas Ambrose, Hamilton College; Valerie Balester, Texas A&M University; Larry Beason, Eastern Washington University; C. Jerome Binus, Butler County Community College; Alisa Branham, University of Kansas; Daniel Cross, Southwest Missouri State University; Louise Dibble, Suffolk Community College; Michael Dinielli, Chaffey College; Darlynn R. Fink, Clarion University of Pennsylvania; Kim Flachman, California State University, Bakersfield; Charles S. Green, University of Wisconsin, Whitewater; Ted E. Johnston, El Paso Community College; Nancy Joseph, York College of Pennsylvania; Martha Kearns, University of Nevada, Reno; Anne Kozak, College of the Atlantic; Miles S. McCrimmon, J. Sargeant Reynolds Community College; Marshall Meyers, Texas Tech University; Elizabeth Nelson, Saint Peter's College; John Osborne, Butte College; Thea Petchler, University of Minnesota; Elizabeth Renfro, California State University, Chico; Tunis Romein, Charleston Southern University; Richard Sax, Madonna University; Carl Schaeffer, University of Connecticut; Susan Belasco Smith, University of Tulsa; Barbara Y. Stewart, Swarthmore College; Ginnie Streamer, Dundalk Community College; David Takacs, Cornell University; Sharon K. Tetly, University of Idaho; Nora Wagner, University of Akron; Colin Wells, Rutgers University; and Rana K. Williamson, Texas Christian University. Many thanks to all of these teachers for their constructive suggestions.

Thanks also to Andrew Christensen and to my friends at and around Longman, especially Patricia Rossi, Thomas Maeglin, Lynne Cattafi, Robert Ginsberg, and Dorothy Bungert.

The
LITTLE, BROWN
ESSENTIAL HANDBOOK
for
WRITERS

I
CLARITY AND STYLE

1. **Coordination and Subordination** *2*
2. **Parallelism** *4*
3. **Variety and Details** *6*
4. **Appropriate Words** *8*
5. **Exact Words** *11*
6. **Conciseness** *13*

1

COORDINATION AND SUBORDINATION

When clearly written, your sentences show the relationships between ideas and stress the more important ideas over the lesser ones. Two techniques, coordination and subordination, can help you achieve such clarity.

1a. Coordination for relationships

Use COORDINATION to show that two or more elements in a sentence are equally important in meaning.

- Link two complete sentences (main clauses°) with a comma and a coordinating conjunction° (*and, but, or, nor, for, so, yet*).

  Independence Hall in Philadelphia is now restored, but *fifty years ago it was in bad shape.*

- Link two main clauses with a semicolon alone or a semicolon and a conjunctive adverb,° such as *however, indeed,* or *therefore.*

  The building was standing; however, *it suffered from decay and vandalism.*

- Within clauses, link words and word groups with a coordinating conjunction (*and, but, or, nor*) but no comma.

  The people and *officials of the nation* were indifferent to Independence Hall or *took it for granted.*

Coordination clarifies meaning and smooths choppy sentences.

> **CHOPPY SENTENCES** We should not rely so heavily on oil. Coal and uranium are also overused. We have a substantial energy resource in the moving waters of our rivers. Smaller streams add to the total volume of water. The resource renews itself. Coal and oil are irreplaceable. Uranium is also irreplaceable. The cost of water does not increase much over time. The costs of coal, oil, and uranium rise dramatically.

°The degree sign (°) marks every term defined in the Glossary of Terms, beginning on page 151.

1b

IDEAS COORDINATED   We should not rely so heavily on coal, oil, and uranium, for we have a substantial energy resource in the moving waters of our rivers and streams. Coal, oil, and uranium are irreplaceable and thus subject to dramatic cost increases; water, however, is self-renewing and more stable in cost.

NOTES A string of main clauses connected by *and* implies that all ideas are equally important and creates a dull, plodding rhythm. Use subordination (see the next section) to revise such excessive coordination.

Two punctuation errors, the comma splice and the fused sentence, can occur when you link main clauses. See pages 48–50.

1b. Subordination for emphasis

Use SUBORDINATION to indicate that some elements in a sentence are less important than others for your meaning. Usually, the main idea appears in the main clause,° and supporting information appears in subordinate structures such as the following:

• Subordinate clauses° containing a subject and a verb (like a complete sentence) but beginning with a subordinating word such as *although, because, before, if, since, that, when, where, which,* or *who (whom)*.

Although production costs have declined, they are still high. [Stresses that costs are still high.]

Costs, *which* include labor and facilities, are difficult to control. [Stresses that costs are difficult to control.]

• Phrases.°

Despite some decline, production costs are still high.

Costs, *including labor and facilities,* are difficult to control.

• Single words.

Declining costs have not matched prices.
Labor costs are difficult to control.

Subordination can transform a monotonous string of main clauses into a more emphatic and interesting passage. (See also p. 6.)

4 • Parallelism

STRING OF MAIN CLAUSES	In recent years computer prices have fallen, and production costs have fallen more slowly, and computer manufacturers have had to struggle, for their profits have been shrinking.
REVISED	*Because* production costs have fallen more slowly *than computer prices* in recent years, computer manufacturers have had to struggle *with shrinking profits.*

Generally, subordinate clauses give the most emphasis to secondary information, phrases give less, and single words give the least.

NOTE A subordinate clause or a phrase is not a complete sentence and should not be set off and punctuated as one. See pages 47–48 on sentence fragments.

2
PARALLELISM

PARALLELISM is a technique for matching the form of your sentence to its meaning: when your ideas are equally important, or parallel, you express them in similar, or parallel, grammatical form.

> The air is dirtied by *factories belching smoke*
> and
> *vehicles spewing exhaust.*

To spot elements that should be parallel, look for two or more words or phrases connected by coordinating conjunctions or correlative conjunctions, as shown in the sections following.

NOTE Parallelism can work like glue to link and stress the sentences of a paragraph as well as the parts of a sentence: *Pulleys are ancient machines for transferring power. Unfortunately, they are also inefficient machines.*

2a. Parallelism with *and, but, or, nor, yet*

The coordinating conjunctions° *and, but, or, nor,* and *yet* signal a need for parallelism.

The industrial base is *shifting* <u>and</u> *shrinking.*

Politicians seldom *acknowledge the problem* <u>or</u> *propose alternatives.*

Industrial workers are understandably disturbed *that they are losing their jobs* <u>and</u> *that no one seems to care*.

FAULTY Three reasons why steel companies kept losing money were that their plants were inefficient, high labor costs, <u>and</u> foreign competition was increasing.

REVISED Three reasons why steel companies kept losing money were *inefficient plants*, *high labor costs*, and *increasing foreign competition*.

NOTES As the preceding example shows, parallel elements match in structure, but they need not match word for word.

Be careful not to omit needed words in parallel structures.

FAULTY Many workers find it difficult to have faith and work for the future.

REVISED Many workers find it difficult to have faith *in* and work for the future. [*Faith* and *work* require different prepositions,° so both must be stated.]

2b. Parallelism with *both . . . and, either . . . or,* and so on

Correlative conjunctions° stress equality and balance between elements. Parallelism confirms the equality. The correlative conjunctions include *both . . . and, either . . . or, neither . . . nor, not only . . . but also,* and *whether . . . or.*

At the end of the novel, Huck Finn <u>both</u> *rejects society's values by turning down money and a home* <u>and</u> *affirms his own values by setting out for "the territory."*

With correlative conjunctions, the element after the second connector must match the element after the first connector.

FAULTY Huck Finn learns <u>not only</u> that human beings have an enormous capacity for folly <u>but also</u> enormous dignity. [The first element includes *that human beings have;* the second element does not.]

REVISED Huck Finn learns that human beings have *not only an enormous capacity for folly* but also enormous dignity. [Repositioning *not only* makes the two elements parallel.]

3
VARIETY AND DETAILS

To make your writing interesting as well as clear, use varied sentences that are well textured with details.

3a. Varied sentence lengths and structures

In most contemporary writing, sentences tend to vary from about ten to about forty words, with an average of fifteen to twenty-five words. If your sentences are all at one extreme or the other, your readers may have difficulty focusing on main ideas and seeing the relations among them.

- If most of your sentences contain thirty-five words or more, you probably need to break some of them into shorter, simpler sentences.
- If most of your sentences contain fewer than ten or fifteen words, you probably need to add details to them (facing page) or combine them through coordination (p. 2) and subordination (p. 3).

A good way to hold readers' attention is to vary the structure of sentences so that they do not all follow the same pattern, like soldiers in a parade. Some suggestions:

- Enliven strings of main clauses° by subordinating the less important information (italics in the revision below).

MONOTONOUS   The moon is now drifting away from the earth. It moves away at the rate of about one inch a year. Our days on earth are getting longer, and they grow a thousandth of a second longer every century. A month will someday be forty-seven of our present days long, and we might eventually lose the moon altogether. Such great planetary movement rightly concerns astronomers, but it need not worry us. It will take 50 million years.

REVISED   The moon is now drifting away from the earth *at the rate of about one inch a year. At a thousandth of a second or so every century,* our days on earth are getting longer. A month will someday be forty-seven of our present days long, *if we don't eventually lose the moon altogether*. Such great planetary movement rightly concerns astronomers, but it need not worry us. It will take 50 million years.

• Vary the beginnings of sentences so that some do not begin with their subjects.°

Monotonous	The lawyer cross-examined the witness for two days. The witness had expected to be dismissed within an hour and was visibly irritated. He did not cooperate. He was reprimanded by the judge.
Revised	*For two days,* the lawyer cross-examined the witness. *Expecting to be dismissed within an hour,* the witness was visibly irritated. He did not cooperate. *Indeed,* he was reprimanded by the judge.

• Occasionally, to achieve special emphasis, reverse the usual word order of a sentence.

A dozen witnesses testified, and the defense attorney barely questioned eleven of them. *The twelfth, however, he grilled.* [Compare normal word order: *He grilled the twelfth, however.*]

3b. Details

Relevant details such as facts and examples create the texture and life that keep readers awake and help them grasp your meaning. For instance:

Flat	Constructed after World War II, Levittown, New York, comprised thousands of houses in two basic styles. Over the decades, residents have altered the houses so dramatically that the original styles are often unrecognizable.
Detailed	Constructed *on potato fields* after World War II, Levittown, New York, comprised *more than 17,000* houses in *Cape Cod and ranch* styles. Over the decades, residents have *added expansive columned porches, punched dormer windows through roofs, converted garages to sun porches, and otherwise* altered the houses so dramatically that the original styles are often unrecognizable.

4

APPROPRIATE WORDS

A country as diverse as the United States naturally encompasses varied subcultures with their own rich and vital vocabularies, such as the dialects of many African-Americans and Hawaiians or the technical slang of computer hackers. The common language that brings all speakers together is STANDARD ENGLISH, usually defined as the English expected and used by educated readers and writers. Standard English is "standard" not because it is better than other forms of English but because it is accepted as the common language, much as dimes and quarters are accepted as the common currency. Standard English allows diverse people to communicate.

In situations calling for standard English, including most academic and business writing, you should use some specialized vocabularies only cautiously, as when aiming for a particular effect with an audience you know will appreciate it. You should entirely avoid some other vocabularies, especially those expressing prejudice, out of consideration for your readers' feelings.

4a. Slang

SLANG is the insider language used by a group, such as musicians or football players, to reflect common experiences and to make technical references efficient. The following example is from an essay on the slang of "skaters" (skateboarders):

> Curtis slashed ultra-punk crunchers on his longboard, while the Rube-man flailed his usual Gumbyness on tweaked frontsides and lofty fakie ollies.
> —MILES ORKIN, "Mucho Slingage by the Pool"

Though valuable within a group, slang is often too private or imprecise for academic or business writing.

4b. Colloquial language

COLLOQUIAL LANGUAGE is the everyday spoken language, including expressions such as *get together*, *go crazy*, and *do the dirty work*. It is labeled "informal" or "colloquial" in your dictionary.

Colloquial language suits informal writing, and an occasional colloquial word can help you achieve a desired emphasis in otherwise formal writing. But most colloquial language is not precise enough for academic or career writing.

4c. Dialect

Like many countries, the United States includes scores of regional, social, or ethnic groups with their own distinct DIALECTS, or versions of English: standard English, Black English, Appalachian English, and Creole are examples. All the dialects of English share many features, but each also has its own vocabulary, pronunciation, and grammar.

If you speak a dialect of English besides standard English, you need to be careful about using your dialect in situations where standard English is the norm, such as in academic or business writing. Otherwise, your readers may not understand your meaning, or they may perceive your usage as incorrect. (Dialects are not wrong in themselves, but forms imported from one dialect into another may still be perceived as wrong.)

Edit your drafts carefully to eliminate dialect expressions, especially those which dictionaries label "nonstandard," such as *hisn, hern, hisself, theirselves, them books, them courses, this here school, that there building, knowed, throwed, hadn't ought, could of, didn't never,* and *haven't no.*

4d. Technical words

All disciplines and professions rely on specialized language that allows the members to communicate precisely and efficiently with each other. Chemists, for instance, have their *phosphatides,* and literary critics have their *subtexts.* When writing to a nonspecialist audience, avoid unnecessary technical terms and carefully define necessary terms.

4e. Indirect and pretentious writing

Small, plain, and direct words are usually preferable to big, showy, or evasive words. Take special care to avoid the following:

4f

- EUPHEMISMS are presumably inoffensive words that substitute for words deemed potentially offensive or too blunt, such as *passed away* for *died* or *misspeak* for *lie*. Use euphemisms only when you know that blunt, truthful words would needlessly hurt or offend members of your audience.
- DOUBLE TALK (at times called DOUBLESPEAK or WEASEL WORDS) is language intended to confuse or to be misunderstood: the *revenue enhancement* that is really a tax, the *biodegradable* bags that last decades. Double talk has no place in honest writing.
- PRETENTIOUS WRITING is fancy language that is more elaborate than its subject requires. Choose your words for their exactness and economy. The big, ornate word may be tempting, but pass it up. Your readers will be grateful.

PRETENTIOUS	Many institutions of higher education recognize the need for youth at the threshold of maturity to confront the choice of life's endeavor and thus require students to select a field of concentration.
REVISED	Many colleges and universities force students to make decisions about their careers by requiring them to select a major.

4f. Sexist and other biased language

Language can reflect and perpetuate inaccurate and hurtful prejudices toward groups of people, especially racial, ethnic, religious, age, and sexual groups. Insulting language communicates nothing but insult and reflects more poorly on the user than on the person or persons designated. Unbiased language does not submit to stereotypes. It refers to people as they would wish to be referred to.

Among the most subtle and persistent biased language is sexist language that distinguishes needlessly between men and women in such matters as behavior, ability, temperament, occupation, and maturity. The following guidelines can help you eliminate sexist language from your writing:

- Avoid demeaning and patronizing language—for instance, identifying women and men differently or trivializing either gender.

SEXIST	President Reagan came to Nancy's defense.
REVISED	President Reagan came to *Mrs. Reagan's* defense.

SEXIST   Ladies are entering almost every occupation.

REVISED   *Women* are entering almost every occupation.

5

• Avoid occupational or social stereotypes, assuming that a role or profession is exclusively male or female.

SEXIST   The considerate doctor commends a nurse when she provides his patients with good care.

REVISED   The considerate doctor commends a nurse *who provides good care for patients*.

• Avoid using *man* or words containing *man* to refer to all human beings. Some alternatives:

businessman	businessperson
chairman	chair, chairperson
congressman	representative in Congress, legislator
craftsman	craftsperson, artisan
layman	layperson
mankind	humankind, humanity, human beings, people
manpower	personnel, human resources
policeman	police officer
salesman	salesperson, sales representative

SEXIST   Man has not reached the limits of social justice.

REVISED   *Humankind* (or *Humanity*) has not reached the limits of social justice.

SEXIST   The furniture consists of manmade materials.

REVISED   The furniture consists of *synthetic* materials.

• Avoid using *he* to refer to both genders. (See also p. 36.)

SEXIST   The newborn child explores his world.

REVISED   The newborn child explores *his or her* world. [Male and female pronouns.]

REVISED   Newborn *children* explore *their* world. [Plural.]

REVISED   The newborn child explores *the* world. [Pronoun avoided.]

5

EXACT WORDS

To write clearly and effectively, you will want to find the words that fit your meaning exactly and convey your attitude precisely.

5a. The right word for your meaning

One key to helping readers understand you is to use words according to their established meanings.

- Become acquainted with a dictionary. Consult it whenever you are unsure of a word's meaning.
- Distinguish between similar-sounding words that have widely different meanings.

INEXACT   Older people often suffer *infirmaries* [places for the sick].

EXACT   Older people often suffer *infirmities* [disabilities].

Some words, called HOMONYMS, sound exactly alike but differ in meaning: for example, *principal/principle* or *rain/reign/rein*. (Many homonyms and near-homonyms are listed in the Glossary of Usage, p. 139.)

- Distinguish between words with related but distinct meanings.

INEXACT   Television commercials *continuously* [unceasingly] interrupt programming.

EXACT   Television commercials *continually* [regularly] interrupt programming.

- Distinguish between words that have similar basic meanings but different emotional associations, or CONNOTATIONS.

It is a *daring* plan. [The plan is bold and courageous.]
It is a *reckless* plan. [The plan is thoughtless and risky.]

Many dictionaries list and distinguish such SYNONYMS, words with approximately, but often not exactly, the same meanings.

5b. Concrete and specific words

Clear, exact writing balances abstract and general words, which outline ideas and objects, with concrete and specific words, which sharpen and solidify.

- ABSTRACT WORDS name qualities and ideas: *beauty, inflation, management, culture, liberal.* CONCRETE WORDS name things we can know by our five senses of sight, hearing, touch, taste, and smell: *sleek, humming, brick, bitter, musty.*
- GENERAL WORDS name classes or groups of things, such as *buildings, weather,* or *birds,* and include all the vari-

eties of the class. SPECIFIC WORDS limit a general class, such as *buildings,* by naming one of its varieties, such as *skyscraper, Victorian courthouse,* or *hut.*

Abstract and general statements need development with concrete and specific details. For example:

VAGUE The size of his hands made his smallness real. [How big were his hands? How small was he?]

EXACT Not until I saw his white, doll-like hands did I realize that he stood a full head shorter than most other men.

5c. Idioms

IDIOMS are expressions in any language that do not fit the rules for meaning or grammar—for instance, *put up with, plug away at, make off with.*

Because they are not governed by rules, idioms usually cause particular difficulty for people learning to speak and write a new language. But even native speakers of English misuse some idioms involving prepositions,° such as *agree on a plan, agree to a proposal,* and *agree with a person* or *charge for a purchase* and *charge with a crime.*

When in doubt about an idiom, consult your dictionary under the main word (*agree* and *charge* in the examples). (See also pp. 31–32 on verbs with particles.)

5d. Trite expressions

TRITE EXPRESSIONS, or CLICHÉS, are phrases so old and so often repeated that they have become stale. Examples include *better late than never, beyond the shadow of a doubt, face the music, green with envy, ladder of success, point with pride, sneaking suspicion,* and *wise as an owl.*

Clichés may slide into your drafts. In editing be wary of any expression you have heard or used before. Substitute fresh words of your own, or restate the idea in plain language.

6
CONCISENESS

Concise writing makes every word count. Conciseness is not the same as mere brevity: detail and originality should not be cut with needless words. Rather, the length of an expression should be appropriate to the thought.

You may find yourself writing wordily when you are unsure of your subject or when your thoughts are tangled. It's fine, even necessary, to stumble and grope while drafting. But you should straighten out your ideas and eliminate wordiness during revision and editing.

6a. Focusing on the subject and verb

The heart of every sentence is its subject,° which names who or what the sentence is about, and its verb,° which specifies what the subject does or is. When the subject and verb do not identify the key actor and action, the sentence is bound to be wordy. In the examples below, the subjects and verbs are italicized.

> **WORDY**   The *occurrence* of the winter solstice, the shortest day of the year, *is* an event occurring about December 22.

> **REVISED**   The winter *solstice*, the shortest day of the year, *occurs* about December 22.

Focusing on the subject and verb can help you with most of the editing techniques discussed below.

6b. Cutting empty words

Cutting words that contribute nothing to your meaning will make your writing move faster and work harder.

> **WORDY**   As far as I am concerned, because of the fact that a situation of discrimination continues to exist in the field of medicine, women have not at the present time achieved equality with men.

> **CONCISE**   Because of continuing discrimination in medicine, women have not yet achieved equality with men.

Some empty expressions can be cut entirely, such as *all things considered, a person by the name of, as far as I'm concerned, for all intents and purposes, in a manner of speaking,* and *more or less.* Others can also be cut, usually along with some of the words around them: *area, aspect, case, element, factor, field, kind, manner, nature, situation, thing, type.* Still others can be reduced from several words to a single word—for instance, *at the present time* and *in today's society* both reduce to *now.*

6c. Cutting unneeded repetition

Unnecessary repetition weakens sentences and paragraphs.

WORDY   Many unskilled workers *without training in a particular job* are unemployed *and do not have any work*. These *unskilled workers* depend on government aid.

CONCISE   Many unskilled workers are unemployed. *They* depend on government aid.

Be especially alert to phrases that say the same thing twice. In the following examples, only the underlined words are needed: *circle around, consensus of opinion, co-operate together, dead body, final completion, the future to come, important (basic) essentials, repeat again, return again, square (round) in shape, surrounding circumstances.*

6d. Reducing clauses and phrases

Modifiers° can be expanded or contracted depending on the emphasis you want to achieve. (Generally, the longer a construction, the more emphasis it has.) When editing your sentences, consider whether any modifiers can be reduced without loss of emphasis or clarity.

WORDY   The Channel Tunnel, *which links Britain and France,* bores through *a bed of solid chalk that is twenty-three miles across.*

REVISED   The Channel Tunnel *linking Britain and France* bores through *twenty-three miles of solid chalk.*

6e. Using strong verbs

Weak verbs such as *is, has,* and *make* stall sentences and usually carry the extra baggage of unneeded or vague words.

WORDY   The drillers *made slow advancement,* and costs *were over* $5 million a day. The slow progress *was worrisome for* backers, who *had had expectations of* high profits.

CONCISE   The drillers *advanced slowly,* and costs *topped* $5 million a day. The slow progress *worried* backers, who *had expected* high profits.

6f. Using the active voice

In the verb's active voice,° the verb's subject names the performer of the verb's action (*banks underline{invested}*). In the passive voice,° in contrast, the verb's subject names the receiver of the verb's action (*funds underline{were invested}*). (See pp. 26–27 for more on the construction of the active and passive voice.)

The active voice is usually clearer and more concise than the passive voice. Reserve the passive voice mainly for emphasizing the receiver rather than the performer of the verb's action.

WORDY PASSIVE	Up to *fifteen feet* of chalk an hour *were devoured* by the drill.
CONCISE ACTIVE	The *drill devoured* up to fifteen feet of chalk an hour.

6g. Cutting *there is* or *it is*

Sentences beginning *there is* or *it is* (called expletive constructions°) are sometimes useful to emphasize a change in direction, but usually they just add needless words.

WORDY	*There are more than half a million shareholders who* have invested in the tunnel. *It is they and the banks that* hope to profit now that the tunnel is open.
CONCISE	*More than half a million shareholders* have invested in the tunnel. *They and the banks* hope to profit now that the tunnel is open.

6h. Combining sentences

Often the information in two or more sentences can be combined into one tight sentence.

WORDY	So far, business has been disappointing. Fewer travelers than were expected have boarded the tunnel train. The train runs between London and Paris.
REVISED	So far, business has been disappointing, with fewer travelers than expected boarding the tunnel train between London and Paris.

II
SENTENCE PARTS AND PATTERNS

VERBS

7. Forms *18*
8. Tenses *21*
9. Mood *25*
10. Voice *26*
11. Agreement of Subject and Verb *27*
12. Other Complications ESL *30*

PRONOUNS

13. Forms *33*
14. Agreement of Pronoun and Antecedent *35*
15. Reference of Pronoun to Antecedent *37*

MODIFIERS

16. Adjectives and Adverbs *40*
17. Misplaced and Dangling Modifiers *44*

SENTENCE FAULTS

18. Fragments *47*
19. Comma Splices and Fused Sentences *48*

7
VERB FORMS

7b

Verb forms may give you trouble when the verb is irregular, when you omit certain endings, or when you need to use helping verbs.

7a. *Sing/sang/sung* and other irregular verbs

Most verbs are REGULAR: their past-tense form° and past participle° end in *-d* or *-ed:*

Today the birds *migrate.* They *soar.* [Plain form° of verb.]

Yesterday the birds *migrated.* They *soared.* [Past-tense form.]

In the past the birds have *migrated.* They have *soared.* [Past participle.]

About two hundred IRREGULAR VERBS in English create their past-tense form and past participle in some way besides adding *-d* or *-ed.* These irregular verbs include *become* (*became/become*), *begin* (*began/begun*), *give* (*gave/given*), and *sing* (*sang/sung*).

Today the birds *fly.* They *begin* migration. [Plain form.]

Yesterday the birds *flew.* They *began* migration. [Past-tense form.]

In the past the birds have *flown.* They have *begun* migration. [Past participle.]

Check a dictionary under a verb's plain form if you have any doubt about the verb's other forms. If the verb is regular, the dictionary will follow the plain form with the *-d* or *-ed* form. If the verb is irregular, the dictionary will follow the plain form with the past-tense form and then the past participle. If the dictionary gives only one irregular form after the plain form, the past-tense form and past participle are the same (*think, thought, thought*).

7b. *-s* and *-ed* verb endings

Speakers of some English dialects and nonnative speakers of English sometimes omit verb endings that are required by standard English. One is the *-s* ending on the verb when the subject° is *he, she, it,* or a singular noun° and the verb's action occurs in the present.

> The letter *asks* (not *ask*) for a quick response.
> The company *has* (not *have*) delayed responding.
> The treasurer *doesn't* (not *don't*) have the needed data.
> Delay *is* (not *be*) costly.

A second omitted ending is the *-d* or *-ed* needed when (1) the verb's action occurred in the past (*we bagged*), (2) the verb form functions as a modifier° (*used cars*), or (3) the verb form combines with a form of *be* or *have* (*was supposed, has asked*).

> The company *used to* (not *use to*) be more responsive.

> We *provided* (not *provide*) the *requested* (not *request*) data as soon as we were *asked* (not *ask*).

> We were *supposed* (not *suppose*) to be the best in the industry.

7c. Helping verbs + main verbs ESL

Helping verbs° combine with main verbs° in specific ways.

Form of *be* + present participle

Create the progressive tenses° with *be, am, is, are, was, were,* or *been* followed by the main verb's present participle° (ending in *-ing*).

> She *is working* on a new book.

Be and *been* require additional helping verbs to form progressive tenses.

can	might	should		have	
could	must	will	}*be* working	has	}*been* working
may	shall	would		had	

When forming the progressive tenses, be sure to use the *-ing* form of the main verb.

NOTE Verbs that express mental states or activities rather than physical actions do not usually appear in the progressive tenses. These verbs include *adore, appear, believe, belong, have, hear, know, like, love, need, see, taste, think, understand,* and *want*.

7c

FAULTY	She *is wanting* to understand contemporary ethics.
REVISED	She *wants* to understand contemporary ethics.

Form of *be* + past participle

Create the passive voice° with *be, am, is, are, was, were, being,* or *been* followed by the main verb's past participle° (usually ending in *-d* or *-ed* or, for irregular verbs, in *-t* or *-n*).

Her latest book *was completed* in four months.
It *was brought* to the President's attention.

Be, being, and *been* require additional helping verbs to form the passive voice.

$$\left.\begin{array}{l} \text{have} \\ \text{has} \\ \text{had} \end{array}\right\} \textit{been } \text{completed} \qquad \left.\begin{array}{ll} \text{am} & \text{was} \\ \text{is} & \text{were} \\ \text{are} \end{array}\right\} \textit{being } \text{completed}$$

will *be* completed

Be sure to use the main verb's past participle for the passive voice.

NOTE Use only transitive verbs° to form the passive voice.

FAULTY	A philosophy conference *was occurred* that week. [*Occur* is not a transitive verb.]
REVISED	A philosophy conference *occurred* that week.

Form of *have* + past participle

Four forms of *have* serve as helping verbs: *have, has, had, having.* One of these forms plus the main verb's past participle creates one of the perfect tenses.°

Some students *have complained* about the laboratory.
Others *had complained* before.

Will and other helping verbs sometimes accompany forms of *have* in the perfect tenses.

Several more students *will have complained* by the end of the week.

Form of *do* + plain form

Always with the plain form° of the main verb, three forms of *do* serve as helping verbs: *do, does, did.* These forms have three uses:

- To pose a question: *How did the trial end?*
- To emphasize the main verb: *It did end eventually.*
- To negate the main verb, along with *not* or *never: The judge did not withdraw.*

Be sure to use the main verb's plain form with any form of *do.*

Faulty The judge did *remained* in court.

Revised The judge did *remain* in court.

Modal + plain form

The MODALS are ten helping verbs that never change form.

| can | may | must | shall | will |
| could | might | ought | should | would |

The modals indicate necessity, obligation, permission, possibility, and other meanings. They are always used with the plain form of the main verb.

Most of the students *can speak* English, but they *may struggle* on written tests. *Will* the scores *reflect* their knowledge?

8
VERB TENSES

Definitions and examples of the verb tenses appear on pages 162–63. The following are the most common trouble spots.

8a. Uses of the present tense (*sing*)

Most academic and business writing uses the past tense° (*the rebellion occurred*), but the present tense has several distinctive uses:

ACTION OCCURRING NOW

We *define* the problem differently.

HABITUAL OR RECURRING ACTION

Banks regularly *undergo* audits.

A GENERAL TRUTH

The earth *is* round.

8d

DISCUSSION OF LITERATURE, FILM, AND SO ON

Huckleberry Finn *has* adventures we all envy.

FUTURE TIME

Funding *ends* in less than a year.

8b. Uses of the perfect tenses (*have/had/will have sung*)

The perfect tenses° generally indicate an action completed before another specific time or action. The present perfect tense° also indicates action begun in the past and continued into the present.

present perfect
The dancer *has performed* here only once.

present perfect
Critics *have written* about the performance ever since.

past perfect
The dancer *had trained* in Asia before his performance here ten years ago.

future perfect
He *will have performed* here again by next month.

8c. Consistency in tense

Within a sentence, the tenses of verbs and verb forms need not be identical as long as they reflect actual changes in time: *Ramon will graduate from college twenty years after his father arrived in America.* But needless shifts in tense will confuse or distract readers.

INCONSISTENT	Immediately after Booth *shot* Lincoln, Major Rathbone *threw* himself upon the assassin. But Booth *pulls* a knife and *plunges* it into the major's arm.
REVISED	Immediately after Booth *shot* Lincoln, Major Rathbone *threw* himself upon the assassin. But Booth *pulled* a knife and *plunged* it into the major's arm.

8d. Sequence of tenses

The SEQUENCE OF TENSES is the relation between the verb tense in a main clause° and the verb tense in a subordinate clause.°

Past or past perfect tense in main clause

When the verb in the main clause is in the past tense° or past perfect tense,° the verb in the subordinate clause must also be past or past perfect.

The researchers *discovered* that people *varied* widely in their knowledge of public events.

The variation *occurred* because respondents *had been born* in different decades.

None of them *had been born* when Warren G. Harding *was* President.

EXCEPTION Always use the present tense° for a general truth, such as *The earth is round.*

Few *understood* that popular Presidents *are* not necessarily good Presidents.

Conditional sentences ESL

A CONDITIONAL SENTENCE usually consists of a subordinate clause beginning *if, when,* or *unless* and a main clause stating the result. The three kinds of conditional sentences use distinctive verbs.

* For factual statements that something always or usually happens whenever something else happens, use the present tense in both clauses.

When a voter *casts* a ballot, he or she *has* complete privacy.

If the linked events occurred in the past, use the past tense in both clauses.

When voters *registered* in some states, they *had* to pay a poll tax.

* For predictions, generally use the present tense in the subordinate clause and the future tense° in the main clause.

Unless citizens *regain* faith in politics, they *will* not *vote.*

* For speculations about events that are possible though unlikely, use the past tense in the subordinate clause

8d

and *would, could,* or *might* plus the verb's plain form in the main clause.

If voters *had* more confidence, they *would vote* more often.
       past   would + verb

Use *were* instead of *was* when the subject is *I, he, she, it,* or a singular noun.

If the voter *were* more confident, he or she *would vote* more often.

For events that are impossible now—that are contrary to fact—use the same forms as above (including the distinctive *were* when applicable).

If Lincoln *were* alive, he *might inspire* confidence.

For events that were impossible in the past, use the past perfect tense in the subordinate clause and *would, could,* or *might* plus the present perfect tense° in the main clause.

If Lincoln *had survived* the Civil War, he *might have stabilized* the country.

The last four examples above illustrate the subjunctive mood of verbs. See Chapter 9.

Indirect quotations   ESL

An indirect quotation° usually appears in a subordinate clause, and its verb depends on the verb in the main clause.

When the verb in the main clause is in the present tense, the verb in the indirect quotation (subordinate clause) is in the same tense as the original quotation.

Haworth *says* that Lincoln *is* our noblest national hero. [Quotation: "Lincoln *is* our noblest national hero."]

When the verb in the main clause is in the past tense, the verb in the indirect quotation usually changes tense from the original quotation. Present tense changes to past tense.

An assistant to Lincoln *said* that the President *was* always generous. [Quotation: "The President *is* always generous."]

Past tense and present perfect tense change to past perfect tense. (Past perfect tense does not change.)

$\overset{\text{past}}{\text{Lincoln } said}$ that events $\overset{\text{past perfect}}{had \ controlled}$ him. [Quotation: "Events *have controlled* me."]

9
VERB MOOD

The MOOD of a verb indicates whether a sentence is a statement or a question (*The theater needs help. Can you help the theater?*), a command (*Help the theater*), or a suggestion, desire, or other nonfactual expression (*I wish I were an actor*).

9a. Consistency in mood

Shifts in mood within a sentence or among related sentences can be confusing. Such shifts occur most frequently in directions.

INCONSISTENT	Dissolve the crystals in the liquid. Then you should heat the solution to 120°C.
REVISED	Dissolve the crystals in the liquid. Then *heat* the solution to 120°C.

9b. Subjunctive mood: *I wish I were*

The SUBJUNCTIVE MOOD expresses a suggestion, requirement, or desire, or it states a condition that is contrary to fact (that is, imaginary or hypothetical).

- Suggestion or requirement with the verb *ask, insist, urge, require, recommend,* or *suggest:* use the verb's plain form° with all subjects.

  Rules require that every donation *be* mailed.

- Desire or present condition contrary to fact: use the verb's past-tense form;° for *be,* use the past-tense form *were*.

  If the theater *were* in better shape and *had* more money, its future would be guaranteed.

  I wish I *were* able to donate money.

- Past condition contrary to fact: use the verb's past-perfect form° (*had* + past participle).

The theater would be better funded if it *had been* better managed.

NOTE In a sentence expressing a condition contrary to fact, the helping verb° *would* or *could* does not appear in the clause beginning *if*.

| **NOT** | Many people would have helped if they *would have* known. |
| **BUT** | Many people would have helped if they *had* known. |

Notice also that *have,* not *of,* follows *would* or *could:* *would <u>have</u>* (not *<u>of</u>*) *helped*.

10

VERB VOICE

The VOICE of a verb tells whether the subject° of the sentence performs the action (ACTIVE VOICE) or is acted upon (PASSIVE VOICE).

| **ACTIVE VOICE** | Commercial services *expand* participation on the Internet. |
| **PASSIVE VOICE** | Participation on the Internet *is expanded* by commercial services. |

10a. Consistency in voice

A shift in voice (and subject) from one sentence to another can be awkward or even confusing.

| **INCONSISTENT** | Commercial *services provide* fairly inexpensive Internet access, and *navigation is made* easy by their software. |
| **REVISED** | Commercial services provide fairly inexpensive Internet access, and their *software makes* navigation easy. |

10b. Active voice vs. passive voice

The active voice always names the actor in a sentence (whoever performs the verb's action), whereas the passive voice puts the actor in a phrase after the verb or even omits the actor altogether. Thus the active voice is usually more clear, direct, and concise than the passive voice.

WEAK PASSIVE   The *Internet is used* for research by many scholars, and its *expansion* to the general public *has been criticized* by some.

STRONG ACTIVE   Many *scholars use* the Internet for research, and *some have criticized* its expansion to the general public.

The passive voice is useful in two situations: when the actor is unknown and when the actor is unimportant or less important than the object of the action.

11a

The Internet *was established* in 1969 by the U.S. Department of Defense. The network *has* now *been extended* internationally to governments, universities, foundations, corporations, and private individuals. [In the first sentence the writer wishes to stress the Internet rather than the Department of Defense. In the second sentence the actor is unknown or too complicated to name.]

After the solution *had been cooled* to 10°C, the acid *was added*. [The person who cooled and added, perhaps the writer, is less important than the facts that the solution was cooled and acid was added. Passive sentences are common in scientific writing.]

11
AGREEMENT OF SUBJECT
AND VERB

A subject° and its verb° should agree in number° (singular, plural) and person° (first, second, third).

More *Japanese-Americans live* in Hawaii and California
      subject   verb
than elsewhere.

Daniel Inouye was the first Japanese-American in Congress.
subject   verb

11a. Words between subject and verb

A catalog of courses and requirements often *baffles* (not *baffle*) students.

The requirements stated in the catalog *are* (not *is*) unclear.

Phrases beginning with *as well as, together with, along with,* and *in addition to* do not change the number of the subject.

The president, as well as the deans, *has* (not *have*) agreed to revise the catalog.

11b. Subjects with *and*

Frost and Roethke *were* American poets who died in the same year.

NOTE When *each* or *every* precedes the compound subject, the verb is usually singular.

Each man, woman, and child *has* a right to be heard.

11c. Subjects with *or* or *nor*

When parts of a subject are joined by *or* or *nor,* the verb agrees with the nearer part.

Either the painter or the carpenter *knows* the cost.

The cabinets or the bookcases *are* too costly.

When one part of the subject is singular and the other is plural, the sentence will be awkward unless you put the plural part second.

AWKWARD   Neither the owners nor the contractor *agrees.*

IMPROVED   Neither the contractor nor the owners *agree.*

11d. *Everyone* and other indefinite pronouns

Indefinite pronouns° such as *everyone, no one,* and *somebody* are usually singular in meaning, and they take singular verbs.

Something *smells.*   Neither *is* right.

A few indefinite pronouns such as *all, any, none,* and *some* may take a singular or plural verb depending on meaning.

All of the money *is* reserved for emergencies.

All of the funds *are* reserved for emergencies.

11e. *Team* and other collective nouns

A collective noun° such as *team* or *family* takes a singular verb when the group acts as a unit.

The group *agrees* that action is necessary.

But when the group's members act separately, use a plural verb.

The old group *have* gone their separate ways.

11h

11f. *Who, which,* and *that*

When used as subjects, *who, which,* and *that* refer to another word in the sentence. The verb agrees with this other word.

Mayor Garber ought to listen to the people who *work* for her.

Bardini is the only aide who *has* her ear.

Bardini is one of the aides who *work* unpaid. [Of the aides who work unpaid, Bardini is one.]

Bardini is the only one of the aides who *knows* the community. [Of the aides, only one, Bardini, knows the community.]

11g. *News* and other singular nouns ending in *-s*

Singular nouns° ending in *-s* include *athletics, economics, mathematics, news, physics, politics,* and *statistics.*

After so long a wait, the news *has* to be good.

Statistics *is* required of psychology majors.

These words take plural verbs when they describe individual items rather than whole bodies of activity or knowledge.

The statistics *prove* him wrong.

11h. Inverted word order

Is voting a right or a privilege?

Are a right and a privilege the same thing?

There *are* differences between them.

11i. *Is, are,* and other linking verbs

Make a linking verb° agree with its subject, usually the first element in the sentence, not with other words referring to the subject.

12a

The child's sole support *is* her court-appointed guardians.

Her court-appointed guardians *are* the child's sole support.

12
OTHER COMPLICATIONS WITH VERBS ESL

Verbs often combine with other words in idioms° that must be memorized.

12a. Verb + gerund or infinitive

A GERUND is the *-ing* form of a verb used as a noun (*Smoking kills*). An INFINITIVE is the plain form° of the verb plus *to* (*Try to quit*). Gerunds and infinitives may follow certain verbs but not others. And sometimes the use of a gerund or infinitive with the same verb changes the meaning of the verb.

Either gerund or infinitive

A gerund or an infinitive may follow these verbs with no significant difference in meaning: *begin, continue, hate, like, love, start.*

The pump began *working.* The pump began *to work.*

Meaning change with gerund or infinitive

With four verbs—*forget, remember, stop,* and *try*—a gerund has quite a different meaning from an infinitive.

The engineer stopped *watching* the pump. [She no longer watched.]

The engineer stopped *to watch* the pump. [She stopped in order to watch.]

Gerund, not infinitive

Do not use an infinitive after these verbs: *admit, adore, appreciate, avoid, deny, detest, discuss, enjoy, escape, finish, imagine, miss, practice, put off, quit, recall, resist, risk, suggest, tolerate.*

FAULTY   She suggested *to check* the pump.

REVISED   She suggested *checking* the pump.

Infinitive, not gerund

Do not use a gerund after these verbs: *agree, ask, assent, beg, claim, decide, expect, have, hope, manage, mean, offer, plan, pretend, promise, refuse, say, wait, want, wish.*

FAULTY   She decided *checking* the pump.

REVISED   She decided *to check* the pump.

Noun or pronoun + infinitive

The verbs *ask, expect, need, want,* and *would like* may be followed by an infinitive alone or by a noun° or pronoun° and an infinitive. A noun or pronoun changes the meaning.

She expected *to watch.*
She expected *her workers to watch.*

Some verbs *must* be followed by a noun or pronoun before an infinitive: *admonish, advise, allow, cause, command, convince, encourage, instruct, order, persuade, remind, require, tell, warn.*

She instructed *her workers to watch.*

Do not use *to* before the infinitive when it comes after one of the following verbs and a noun or pronoun: *feel, have, hear, let, make* ("force"), *see, watch.*

She let her workers *learn* by observation.

12b. Verb + particle

Some verbs consist of two words: the verb itself and a PARTICLE, a preposition° or adverb° that affects the meaning of the verb, as in *Look up the answer* (research the answer) or *Look over the answer* (check the answer). Many of these two-word verbs are defined in dictionaries.

12b

(There are some three-word verbs, too, such as *put up with* and *run out of*.)

Some two-word verbs may be separated in a sentence; others may not.

Inseparable two-word verbs

Verbs and particles that may not be separated by any other words include the following: *catch on, get along, give in, go out, grow up, keep on, look into, run into, run out of, speak up, stay away, take care of.*

FAULTY Children *grow* quickly *up*.

REVISED Children *grow up* quickly.

Separable two-word verbs

Most two-word verbs that take direct objects° may be separated by the object.

Parents *help out* their children.
Parents *help* their children *out*.

If the direct object is a pronoun,° the pronoun *must* separate the verb from the particle.

FAULTY Parents *help out* them.

REVISED Parents *help* them *out*.

The separable two-word verbs include the following: *call off, call up, fill out, fill up, give away, give back, hand in, help out, look over, look up, pick up, point out, put away, put back, put off, take out, take over, try on, try out, turn down.*

PRONOUNS

13

PRONOUN FORMS

A noun° or pronoun° changes form to show the reader how it functions in a sentence. These forms—called CASES—are SUBJECTIVE (such as *I, she, they, man*), OBJECTIVE (such as *me, her, them, man*), and POSSESSIVE (such as *my, her, their, man's*). A list of the case forms appears on page 152.

13a. Compound subjects and objects: *she and I* vs. *her and me*

Subjects° and objects° consisting of two or more nouns and pronouns have the same case forms as they would if one pronoun stood alone.

compound subject
She and Clinton discussed the proposal.
compound object
The proposal disappointed *her and him*.

To test for the correct form, try one pronoun alone in the sentence. The case form that sounds correct is probably correct for all parts of the compound.

The prize went to (*he, him*) and (*I, me*).
The prize went to *him*.
The prize went to *him and me*.

13b. Subject complements: *it was she*

Both a subject and a subject complement° appear in the same form—the subjective case.

subject
complement
The one who cares most is *she*.

If this construction sounds stilted to you, use the more natural order: <u>*She*</u> *is the one who cares most*.

13c. *Who* vs. *whom*

The choice between *who* and *whom* depends on the use of the word.

Questions

At the beginning of a question use *who* for a subject and *whom* for an object.

subject——
Who wrote the policy?

object←
Whom does it affect?

Test for the correct form by answering the question with the form of *he* or *she* that sounds correct. Then use the same form in the question.

(*Who, Whom*) does one ask?
One asks *her.*
Whom does one ask?

Subordinate clauses

In subordinate clauses° use *who* and *whoever* for all subjects, *whom* and *whomever* for all objects.

subject——
Give old clothes to *whoever* needs them.

object←
I don't know *whom* the mayor appointed.

Test for the correct form by rewriting the subordinate clause as a sentence. Replace *who* or *whom* with the form of *he* or *she* that sounds correct. Then use the same form in the original subordinate clause.

Few people know (*who, whom*) they should ask.
They should ask *her.*
Few people know *whom* they should ask.

NOTE Don't let expressions such as *I think* and *she says* confuse you when they come between the subject *who* and its verb.

subject——
He is the one *who* I think is best qualified.

13d. Other constructions

We or *us* with a noun

The choice of *we* or *us* before a noun depends on the use of the noun.

object of
preposition →
Freezing weather is welcomed by *us* skaters.

subject——
We skaters welcome freezing weather.

Pronoun in an appositive

An APPOSITIVE is a word or word group that renames a noun or pronoun. Within an appositive the form of a pronoun depends on the function of the word the appositive renames.

object of verb
The class elected two representatives, DeShawn and *me*.

subject
Two representatives, DeShawn and *I*, were elected.

Pronoun after *than* or *as*

After *than* or *as* in a comparison, the form of a pronoun indicates what words may have been omitted. A subjective pronoun must be the subject of the omitted verb:

subject
Some critics like Glass more than *she* (does).

An objective pronoun must be the object of the omitted verb:

object
Some critics like Glass more than (they like) *her*.

Subject and object of an infinitive

An INFINITIVE is the plain form° of the verb plus *to* (*to swim*). Both its object and its subject are in the objective form.

subject of
infinitive
The school asked *him* to speak.

object of
infinitive
Students chose to invite *him*.

Form before a gerund

A GERUND is the *-ing* form of a verb used as a noun (*a runner's breathing*). Generally, use the possessive form of a pronoun or noun immediately before a gerund.

The coach disapproved of *their* lifting weights.

The *coach's* disapproving was a surprise.

14

AGREEMENT OF PRONOUN
AND ANTECEDENT

The ANTECEDENT of a pronoun° is the noun° or other pronoun it refers to.

Homeowners fret over *their* tax bills.
antecedent   pronoun

Its amount makes the tax *bill* a dreaded document.
pronoun   antecedent

For clarity, a pronoun should agree with its antecedent in person° (first, second, third), number° (singular, plural), and gender° (masculine, feminine, neuter).

14a. Antecedents with *and*

The dean and my adviser have offered *their* help.

NOTE When *each* or *every* precedes the compound antecedent, the pronoun is singular.

Every girl and woman took *her* seat.

14b. Antecedents with *or* or *nor*

When parts of an antecedent are joined by *or* or *nor*, the pronoun agrees with the nearer part.

Tenants or owners must present *their* grievances.

Either the tenant or the owner will have *her* way.

When one subject is plural and the other singular, put the plural subject second to avoid awkwardness.

AWKWARD   Neither the tenants nor the owner has yet made *her* case.

REVISED   Neither the owner nor the tenants have yet made *their* case.

14c. *Everyone* and other indefinite pronouns

Most indefinite pronouns,° such as *anybody* and *everyone*, are singular in meaning. When they serve as antecedents to other pronouns, the other pronouns are also singular.

Everyone on the team had *her* own locker.

Each of the boys likes *his* teacher.

NOTE Tradition has called for *he* to refer to indefinite pronouns and other indefinite words (*child, adult, indi-*

vidual, person), even when both masculine and feminine genders are intended. But increasingly this so-called generic (or generalized) *he* is considered inaccurate or unfair because it excludes females. To avoid it, try one of the following techniques.

> **GENERIC *HE***   Nobody in the class had the credits *he* needed.

* Substitute *he or she*.

> **REVISED**   Nobody in the class had the credits *he or she* needed.

To avoid awkwardness, don't use *he or she* more than once in several sentences.

* Recast the sentence using a plural antecedent and pronoun.

> **REVISED**   *All the students* in the class lacked the credits *they* needed.

* Rewrite the sentence to avoid the pronoun.

> **REVISED**   Nobody in the class had the *needed credits*.

14d. *Team* and other collective nouns

Use a singular pronoun with *team, family, group,* or another collective noun° when referring to the group as a unit.

The committee voted to disband *itself*.

When referring to the individual members of the group, use a plural pronoun.

The old group have gone *their* separate ways.

15
REFERENCE OF PRONOUN TO ANTECEDENT

If a pronoun° does not refer clearly to the word it substitutes for (its ANTECEDENT), readers will have difficulty grasping the pronoun's meaning.

15a. Single antecedent

When either of two words can be a pronoun's antecedent, the reference will not be clear.

> **Confusing**   The workers removed all the furniture from the room and cleaned *it*.

Revise such a sentence in one of two ways:

• Replace the pronoun with the appropriate noun.

> **Clear**   The workers removed all the furniture from the room and cleaned *the room* (or *the furniture*).

• Avoid repetition by rewriting the sentence with the pronoun but with only one possible antecedent.

> **Clear**   After removing all the furniture from *it*, the workers cleaned the room.

> **Clear**   The workers cleaned all the furniture after removing *it* from the room.

15b. Close antecedent

A clause° beginning *who, which,* or *that* should generally fall immediately after the word it refers to.

> **Confusing**   Jody found a dress in the attic *that* her aunt had worn.

> **Clear**   In the attic Jody found a dress *that* her aunt had worn.

15c. Specific antecedent

A pronoun should refer to a specific noun° or other pronoun.

Vague *this, that, which,* or *it*

This, that, which, or *it* should refer to a specific noun, not to a whole word group expressing an idea or situation.

> **Confusing**   The British knew little of the American countryside, and they had no experience with the colonists' guerrilla tactics. *This* gave the colonists an advantage.

Clear	The British knew little of the American countryside, and they had no experience with the colonists' guerrilla tactics. This *ignorance and inexperience* gave the colonists an advantage.

Implied nouns

A pronoun cannot refer clearly to a noun that is merely implied by some other word or phrase, such as *news* in *newspaper* or *happiness* in *happy*.

Confusing	In Joan Cohen's advice *she* was not specific.
Clear	*Joan Cohen's advice* was not specific.
Confusing	She spoke once before, but *it* was sparsely attended.
Clear	She spoke once before, but *the speech* was sparsely attended.

Indefinite *it* and *they*

It and *they* should have definite antecedents.

Confusing	In the average television drama *they* present a false picture of life.
Clear	The average television *drama* presents a false picture of life.

15d. Consistency in pronouns

Within a sentence or a group of related sentences, pronouns should be consistent.

Inconsistent	*One* finds when reading that *your* concentration improves with practice, so that *I* now comprehend more in less time.
Revised	*I* find when reading that *my* concentration improves with practice, so that I now comprehend more in less time.

15d

MODIFIERS

16
ADJECTIVES AND ADVERBS

ADJECTIVES modify nouns° (*good* child) and pronouns° (*special* someone). ADVERBS modify verbs° (*see well*), adjectives (*very* happy), other adverbs (*not very*), and whole word groups (*Otherwise, the room was empty*). The only way to tell if a modifier should be an adjective or an adverb is to determine its function in the sentence.

16a. Adjective vs. adverb

Use only adverbs, not adjectives, to modify verbs, adverbs, or other adjectives.

NOT They took each other *serious*. They related *good*.

BUT They took each other *seriously*. They related *well*.

16b. Adjective with linking verb: *felt bad*

A modifier after a verb should be an adjective if it describes the subject,° an adverb if it describes the verb. In the first example below, the linking verb° *felt* connects the subject and an adjective describing the subject.

The sailors felt *bad*.
      linking adjective
      verb

Some sailors fare *badly* in rough weather.
      verb adverb

Good and *well* are frequently confused after verbs.

Decker trained *well*. [Adverb.]

She felt *well*. Her prospects were *good*. [Adjectives.]

16c. Comparison of adjectives and adverbs

Comparison° allows adjectives and adverbs to show degrees of quality or amount by changing form: *red, redder, reddest; awful, more awful, most awful; quickly, less quickly, least quickly*. A dictionary will list the *-er* and *-est* endings if they can be used. Otherwise, use *more* and *most* or *less* and *least*.

Some modifiers are irregular, changing their spelling for comparison: for example, *good, better, best; many, more, most; badly, worse, worst.*

Comparing two or more than two

Use the *-er* form, *more,* or *less* when comparing two items. Use the *-est* form, *most,* or *least* when comparing three or more items.

Of the two tests, the litmus is *better.*
Of all six tests, the litmus is *best.*

Double comparisons

A double comparison combines the *-er* or *-est* ending with the word *more* or *most.* It is redundant.

Chang was the *wisest* (not *most wisest*) person in town.
He was *smarter* (not *more smarter*) than anyone else.

Complete comparisons

A comparison should be complete.

• The comparison should state a relation fully enough to ensure clarity.

UNCLEAR   Car makers worry about their industry more than environmentalists.

CLEAR   Car makers worry about their industry more than environmentalists *do.*

CLEAR   Car makers worry about their industry more than *they worry about* environmentalists.

• The items being compared should in fact be comparable.

ILLOGICAL   The cost of an electric car is greater than a gasoline-powered car. [Illogically compares a cost and a car.]

REVISED   The cost of an electric car is greater than *the cost of* (or *that of*) a gasoline-powered car.

16d. Double negatives

A DOUBLE NEGATIVE is a nonstandard construction in which two negative words cancel each other out. For in-

16d

stance, *Jenny did not feel nothing* asserts that Jenny felt other than nothing, or something.

> **Faulty** The IRS *cannot hardly* audit all tax returns. *None* of its audits *never* touch many cheaters.

> **Revised** The IRS *cannot* audit all tax returns. Its audits *never* touch many cheaters.

16e. Present and past participles as adjectives ESL

Both present participles° and past participles° may serve as adjectives: *a burning house, a burned house.* As in the examples, the two participles usually differ in the time they indicate.

But some present and past participles—those derived from verbs expressing feeling—can have altogether different meanings. The present participle refers to something that causes the feeling: *That was a frightening storm.* The past participle refers to something that experiences the feeling: *They quieted the frightened horses.* Similar pairs include the following: *annoying/annoyed, boring/bored, confusing/confused, exciting/excited, exhausting/exhausted, interesting/interested, pleasing/pleased, satisfying/satisfied, surprising/surprised, tiring/tired, troubling/troubled, worrying/worried.*

16f. Articles: *a, an, the* ESL

Articles° usually trouble native English speakers only in the choice of *a* versus *an: a* for words beginning with consonant sounds (*a bridge, a uniform*), *an* for words beginning with vowel sounds, including silent *h*'s (*an apple, an urge, an hour*).

For nonnative speakers, *a, an,* and *the* can be difficult, because many other languages use such words quite differently or not at all. In English, their uses depend on the kinds of nouns they precede and the context they appear in.

Singular count nouns

A COUNT NOUN names something countable and can form a plural: *glass/glasses, mountain/mountains, child/children, woman/women.*

- *A* or *an* precedes a singular count noun when your reader does not already know its identity, usually because you have not mentioned it before.

A scientist in our chemistry department developed *a* process to strengthen metals. [*Scientist* and *process* are being introduced for the first time.]

• *The* precedes a singular count noun that has a specific identity for your reader, usually because (1) you have mentioned it before, (2) you identify it immediately before or after you state it, (3) it is unique (the only one in existence), or (4) it refers to an institution or facility that is shared by the community.

16f

A scientist in our chemistry department developed a process to strengthen metals. *The* scientist patented *the* process. [*Scientist* and *process* were identified in the preceding sentence.]

The most productive laboratory is *the* research center in the chemistry department. [*Most productive* identifies *laboratory,* and *in the chemistry department* identifies *research center.*]

The sun rises in *the* east. [*Sun* and *east* are unique.]

Many men and women aspire to *the* presidency. [*Presidency* is a shared institution.]

Plural count nouns

A or *an* never precedes a plural noun. *The* does not precede a plural noun that names a general category. *The* does precede a plural noun that names specific representatives of a category.

Men and *women* are different. [*Men* and *women* name general categories.]

The women formed a team. [*Women* refers to specific people.]

Noncount nouns

A NONCOUNT NOUN names something that is not usually considered countable in English and thus does not form a plural. Examples include *advice, cereal, confidence, equipment, evidence, furniture, health, honesty, information, knowledge, lumber, mail, oil, pollution, research, silver, truth, water, weather, work.*

A or *an* never precedes a noncount noun. *The* does precede a noncount noun that names specific representatives of a general category.

Vegetation suffers from drought. [*Vegetation* names a general category.]

The vegetation in the park withered or died. [*Vegetation* refers to specific plants.]

NOTE Many nouns are sometimes count nouns and sometimes noncount nouns.

The library has *a room* for readers. [*Room* is a count noun meaning "walled area."]

The library has *room* for reading. [*Room* is a noncount noun meaning "space."]

Proper nouns

A PROPER NOUN names a particular person, place, or thing and begins with a capital letter: *February, Joe Allen. A* or *an* never precedes a proper noun. *The* does only occasionally, as with oceans (*the Pacific*), regions (*the Middle East*), rivers (*the Snake*), some countries (*the United States*), and some universities (*the University of Texas*).

Garcia lives in *Boulder,* where he attends *the University of Colorado.*

17

MISPLACED AND DANGLING MODIFIERS

For clarity, modifiers generally must fall close to the words they modify.

17a. Misplaced modifiers

A MISPLACED MODIFIER falls in the wrong place in a sentence. It may be awkward, confusing, or even unintentionally funny.

Clear placement

CONFUSING   He served steak to the men *on paper plates.*

REVISED   He served the men steak *on paper plates.*

CONFUSING   Many dogs are killed by automobiles and trucks *roaming unleashed.*

REVISED   Many dogs *roaming unleashed* are killed by automobiles and trucks.

Only and other limiting modifiers

LIMITING MODIFIERS include *almost, even, exactly, hardly, just, merely, nearly, only, scarcely,* and *simply.* They should fall immediately before the word or word group they modify.

UNCLEAR	They *only* saw each other during meals.
REVISED	They saw *only* each other during meals.
REVISED	They saw each other *only* during meals.

17a

Infinitives and other grammatical units

Some grammatical units should generally not be split by long modifiers. For example, a long modifier between subject° and verb° can be awkward and confusing.

AWKWARD	The *wreckers,* soon after they began demolishing the old house, *discovered* a large box of coins.
REVISED	Soon after they began demolishing the old house, the *wreckers discovered* a large box of coins.

A SPLIT INFINITIVE—a modifier placed between *to* and the verb—can be especially awkward and annoys many readers.

AWKWARD	Forecasters expected temperatures *to* not *rise.*
REVISED	Forecasters expected temperatures not *to rise.*

A split infinitive may sometimes be unavoidable without rewriting, though it may still bother some readers.

Several U.S. industries expect *to* more than *triple* their use of robots.

Order of adjectives ESL

English follows distinctive rules for arranging two or three adjectives before a noun. (A string of more than three adjectives before a noun is rare.) Adjectives always precede the noun except when they are subject complements,° and they follow this order:

1. Article or other word marking the noun: *a, an, the, this, Mary's*
2. Word of opinion: *beautiful, disgusting, important, fine*
3. Word about measurement: *small, huge, short, towering*
4. Word about shape: *round, flat, square, triangular*
5. Word about age: *old, young, new, ancient*
6. Word about color: *green, white, black, magenta*
7. Word about origin (nationality, religion, etc.): *European, Iranian, Jewish, Parisian*
8. Word about material: *wooden, gold, nylon, stone*

Examples of this order include *a new state law, all recent business reports,* and *the blue litmus paper.*

17b. Dangling modifiers

A DANGLING MODIFIER does not sensibly modify anything in its sentence.

DANGLING *Passing the building,* the vandalism became visible.

Like most dangling modifiers, this one introduces a sentence, contains a verb form (*passing*), and implies but does not name a subject (whoever is passing). Readers assume that this implied subject is the same as the subject of the sentence (*vandalism*). When it is not, the modifier "dangles" unconnected to the rest of the sentence.

Revise dangling modifiers to achieve the emphasis you want.

• Rewrite the dangling modifier as a complete clause with its own stated subject and verb. Readers can accept different subjects when they are both stated.

DANGLING *Passing the building,* the vandalism became visible.

REVISED *As we passed* the building, the vandalism became visible.

• Change the subject of the sentence to a word the modifier properly describes.

DANGLING *Trying to understand the causes,* vandalism has been extensively studied.

REVISED Trying to understand the causes, *researchers have* extensively *studied* vandalism.

SENTENCE FAULTS

18

SENTENCE FRAGMENTS

A SENTENCE FRAGMENT is part of a sentence that is set off as if it were a whole sentence by an initial capital letter and a final period or other end punctuation. Although writers occasionally use fragments deliberately and effectively, readers perceive most fragments as serious errors in standard English. Use the tests below to ensure that you have linked or separated your ideas both appropriately for your meaning and correctly, without creating sentence fragments.

NOTE ESL Some languages other than English allow the omission of the subject° or the verb.° Except in commands (*Close the door*), English always requires you to state the subject and verb.

18a. Tests for fragments

A word group punctuated as a sentence should pass *all three* of the following tests. If it does not, it is a fragment and needs to be revised.

Test 1: Find the verb.

The verb in a complete sentence can change form as on the left below. A verb form° that cannot change this way (as on the right) cannot serve as a sentence verb.

	COMPLETE SENTENCES	SENTENCE FRAGMENTS
SINGULAR	The baboon *looks*.	The baboon *looking*.
PLURAL	The baboons *look*.	The baboons *looking*.
PRESENT	The baboon *looks*.	
PAST	The baboon *looked*.	The baboon *looking*.
FUTURE	The baboon *will look*.	

Test 2: Find the subject.

The subject of the sentence will usually come before the verb. If there is no subject, the word group is probably a fragment.

FRAGMENT	And eyed the guard nervously.
REVISED	And *he* eyed the guard nervously.

Test 3: Make sure the clause is not subordinate.

A SUBORDINATE CLAUSE begins with either a subordinating conjunction° (such as *because, if, when*) or a relative pronoun° (*who, which, that*). Subordinate clauses serve as parts of sentences, not as whole sentences.

FRAGMENT When the next cage rattled.

REVISED The next cage rattled.

NOTE Questions beginning *who, whom,* or *which* are not sentence fragments: *Who rattled the cage?*

18b. Revision of fragments

Correct sentence fragments in one of two ways depending on the importance of the information in the fragment.

• As in all examples so far, rewrite the fragment as a complete sentence. The information in the fragment will then have the same importance as that in other complete sentences.
• Combine the fragment with the appropriate main clause. The information in the fragment will then be subordinated to that in the main clause.

FRAGMENT The challenger was a newcomer. *Who was unusually fierce.*

REVISED The challenger was a newcomer who was unusually fierce.

19
COMMA SPLICES AND FUSED SENTENCES

When you combine two complete sentences (main clauses°) in one sentence, you need to give readers a clear signal that one clause is ending and the other beginning. In a COMMA SPLICE two main clauses are joined (or spliced) only by a comma, which is usually too weak to signal the link between main clauses.

COMMA SPLICE The ship was huge, its mast stood eighty feet high.

In a FUSED SENTENCE (or RUN-ON SENTENCE) the clauses are not separated at all.

| **FUSED SENTENCE** | The ship was huge its mast stood eighty feet high. |

19a. Main clauses without *and, but, or, nor, for, so, yet*

And, but, or, or another coordinating conjunction° often signals the joining of main clauses. When a sentence with two main clauses lacks this signal (and is thus a comma splice or fused sentence), revise the sentence in one of the following ways:

• Insert a coordinating conjunction when the ideas in the main clauses are closely related and equally important.

| **COMMA SPLICE** | Some laboratory-grown foods taste good, they are nutritious. |
| **REVISED** | Some laboratory-grown foods taste good, *and* they are nutritious. |

In a fused sentence insert a comma and a coordinating conjunction.

| **FUSED SENTENCE** | Chemists have made much progress they still have a way to go. |
| **REVISED** | Chemists have made much progress, *but* they still have a way to go. |

• Insert a semicolon between clauses if the relation between the ideas is very close and obvious without a conjunction.

| **COMMA SPLICE** | Good taste is rare in laboratory-grown vegetables, they are usually bland. |
| **REVISED** | Good taste is rare in laboratory-grown vegetables; they are usually bland. |

• Make the clauses into separate sentences when the ideas expressed are only loosely related.

| **COMMA SPLICE** | Chemistry has contributed to our understanding of foods, many foods such as wheat and beans can be produced in the laboratory. |
| **REVISED** | Chemistry has contributed to our understanding of foods. Many foods such as wheat and beans can be produced in the laboratory. |

- Subordinate one clause to the other when one idea is less important than the other. The subordinate clause will modify something in the main clause.

COMMA SPLICE	The vitamins are adequate, the flavor and color are deficient.
REVISED	*Even though* the vitamins are adequate, the flavor and color are deficient.

19b. Main clauses related by *however, thus, for example,* and so on

Two kinds of words can describe how one main clause relates to another: conjunctive adverbs,° such as *however, instead, meanwhile,* and *thus;* and other transitional expressions,° such as *even so, for example, in fact,* and *of course.* Two main clauses related by all conjunctive adverbs and most transitional expressions must be separated by a period or by a semicolon. The connecting word or phrase is also generally set off by a comma or commas.

COMMA SPLICE	Most Americans refuse to give up unhealthful habits, consequently our medical costs are higher than those of many other countries.
REVISED	Most Americans refuse to give up unhealthful habits. *Consequently,* our medical costs are higher than those of many other countries.
REVISED	Most Americans refuse to give up unhealthful habits; *consequently,* our medical costs are higher than those of many other countries.

To test whether a word or phrase is a conjunctive adverb or transitional expression, try repositioning it in its clause. It can move.

Most Americans refuse to give up unhealthful habits; our medical costs, *consequently,* are higher than those of many other countries.

III
PUNCTUATION

20. End Punctuation *52*

21. The Comma *53*

22. The Semicolon *57*

23. The Colon *59*

24. The Apostrophe *60*

25. Quotation Marks *62*

26. Other Marks *66*

20

END PUNCTUATION

End a sentence with one of three punctuation marks: a period, a question mark, or an exclamation point.

20a. Period for most sentences and some abbreviations

STATEMENTS

The airline went bankrupt.
It no longer flies.

MILD COMMANDS

Think of the possibilities.
See page 27.

INDIRECT QUESTIONS°

The article asks how we can improve math education.
It asks what cost we are willing to pay.

ABBREVIATIONS

p.	Ph.D.	Mr.
Dr.	e.g.	Mrs.
St.	i.e.	Ms.

Periods may be omitted from abbreviations of two or more words written in all-capital letters.

MD	BC	AM	IBM	JFK
BA	AD	PM	USMC	AIDS

NOTE When a sentence ends in an abbreviation with a period, don't add a second period: *The university offers a well-respected Ph.D.*

20b. Question mark for direct questions°

What is the result?
What is the difference between those proposals?

20c. Exclamation point for strong statements and commands

No! We must not lose this election!
"Oh!" she gasped.

NOTE Use exclamation points sparingly, even in informal writing. They can make writing sound overly dramatic.

21
THE COMMA

The comma is the most common punctuation mark inside sentences. Its main uses (and misuses) appear below.

21a. Comma with *and, but, or, nor, for, so, yet*

Between main clauses

Use a comma before *and, but, or, nor, for, so,* and *yet* (the coordinating conjunctions°) when they link complete sentences (main clauses°).

Banks offer many services, *but* they could do more.

Many banks offer investment advice, *and* they help small businesses establish credit.

NOTE The comma goes before, not after, the coordinating conjunction.

Not between words, phrases, or subordinate clauses

Generally, do not use a comma before *and, but, or,* and *nor* when they link elements other than main clauses: words, phrases,° subordinate clauses.°

NOT   One bank *established* special accounts for older depositors, *and counseled* them on investments.

BUT   One bank established special accounts for older depositors and counseled them on investments.

21b. Comma with introductory elements

Use a comma after most elements that begin sentences and are distinct from the main clause.

When a new century nears, futurists multiply.
Fortunately, some news is good.

You may omit the comma after a short introductory element if there's no risk that the reader will run the introductory element and main clause together: <u>*By the year 2000*</u> *we may have reduced pollution.*

NOTE The subject° of a sentence is not an introductory element but a part of the main clause. Thus, do not use a comma to separate the subject and its verb.

NOT   Some *pessimists, may be* disappointed.

BUT   Some pessimists may be disappointed.

21c. Comma or commas with interrupting and concluding elements

Use a comma or commas to set off elements that provide nonessential information—information that could be deleted without altering the basic meaning of the sentence or leaving it too general.

NOTE When nonessential information falls in the middle of the sentence, be sure to use one comma *before* and one *after* it.

Around nonrestrictive elements

A NONRESTRICTIVE ELEMENT adds information about a word in the sentence but does not limit the word to a particular individual or group. Omitting the element may remove incidental details, but it does not affect the sentence's basic meaning.

Hai Nguyen, *who emigrated from Vietnam,* lives in Denver.

His company, *which is ten years old,* studies air and water pollution.

Nguyen's family lives in St. Louis and Chicago, *even though he lives in Denver.*

Nonrestrictive elements may be modifiers, like those above, or APPOSITIVES, words or word groups that rename nouns.

Nguyen's work, *advanced research into air pollution,* keeps him in Denver.

His wife, *Tina Nguyen,* reports for a newspaper in Chicago.

Not around restrictive elements

Do not use commas to set off RESTRICTIVE ELEMENTS, modifiers and appositives containing information essential to the meaning of the sentence. Omitting a restrictive element alters the sentence's meaning substantially, leaving the sentence unclear or too general.

People *who join recycling programs* rarely complain about the extra work.

The programs *that succeed* are often staffed by volunteers.

21c

The label *"Recycle"* on products becomes a command.

Most people recycle *because they believe they have a responsibility to the earth.*

Around absolute phrases

An ABSOLUTE PHRASE consists usually of the *-ing* form of a verb plus a subject for the verb. The phrase modifies the whole main clause of the sentence.

Health insurance, *its cost always rising,* is a concern for many students.

Around parenthetical expressions

A PARENTHETICAL EXPRESSION is a supplemental or transitional word or phrase, such as *of course, however,* or a brief example or fact. It can be enclosed in parentheses (see p. 67) or, with more emphasis, in commas.

Some schools, *it seems,* do not offer group insurance.

Around phrases of contrast

Students may focus on the cost of care, *not their health.*

Around *yes* and *no*

All schools should agree that, *yes,* they will provide at least minimal insurance at low cost.

Around words of direct address

Heed this lesson, *readers.*

21d. Commas with series

Between series items

Use commas to separate the items in lists, or series.

The names *Belial, Beelzebub, and Lucifer* sound ominous.

The comma before the last item in a series (before *and*) is actually optional, but it is never wrong and it is usually clearer.

Not around series

Do not use a comma *before* or *after* a series.

> **Not** The skills of, *agriculture, herding, and hunting,* sustained the Native Americans.

> **But** The skills of agriculture, herding, and hunting sustained the Native Americans.

21e. Comma with adjectives

Between equal adjectives

Use a comma between two or more adjectives° when each one modifies the same word equally. As a test, such adjectives could be joined by *and*.

The *dirty*, *dented* car was a neighborhood eyesore.

Not between unequal adjectives

Do not use a comma between adjectives when one forms a unit with the modified word. As a test, the two adjectives could not sensibly be joined by *and*.

The house overflowed with *ornate electric* fixtures.
Among the junk in the attic was *one lovely* vase.

21f. Commas with dates, addresses, place names, numbers

When they appear within sentences, elements punctuated with commas are also ended with commas.

DATES

July 4, 1776, was the day the Declaration was signed. [Note that commas appear before *and* after the year.]

The United States entered World War II in December 1941. [No comma is needed between a month or season and a year.]

ADDRESSES AND PLACE NAMES

Use the address 806 Ogden Avenue, Swarthmore, Pennsylvania 19081, for all correspondence. [No comma is needed between the state name and zip code.]

NUMBERS

The new assembly plant cost $7,525,000.
A kilometer is 3,281 feet (*or* 3281 feet).

21g. Commas with quotations

A comma or commas usually separate a quotation from the words used to identify the source, such as *she said* or *he replied.*

Eleanor Roosevelt said**,** "You must do the thing you think you cannot do."

"Knowledge is power**,**" wrote Francis Bacon.

"You don't need a weatherman**,**" sings Bob Dylan**,** "to know which way the wind blows."

Do not use a comma when identifying words interrupt the quotation between main clauses.° Instead, follow the identifying words with a semicolon or period.

"That part of my life was over," she wrote**;** "his words had sealed it shut."

"That part of my life was over," she wrote**.** "His words had sealed it shut."

22a

22
THE SEMICOLON

The semicolon separates equal and balanced sentence elements, usually complete sentences (main clauses°).

22a. Semicolon between complete sentences not joined by *and, but, or, nor,* etc.

Between complete sentences

Use a semicolon between complete sentences (main clauses°) that are not connected by *and, but, or, nor, for, so,* or *yet* (the coordinating conjunctions°).

Increased taxes are only one way to pay for programs**;** cost cutting also frees up money.

Not between main clauses and subordinate elements

Do not use a semicolon between a main clause and a subordinate element, such as a subordinate clause° or a phrase.°

NOT	According to African authorities; only about 35,000 Pygmies exist today.
BUT	According to African authorities**,** only about 35,000 Pygmies exist today.

NOT	Anthropologists have campaigned; for the protection of the Pygmies' habitat.
BUT	Anthropologists have campaigned for the protection of the Pygmies' habitat.

22b. Semicolon with *however, thus, for example,* and so on

Use a semicolon between complete sentences (main clauses°) that are related by two kinds of words: conjunctive adverbs,° such as *hence, however, indeed, moreover, therefore,* and *thus;* and other transitional expressions,° such as *after all, for example, in fact,* and *of course.*

Blue jeans have become fashionable all over the world**;** *however,* the American originators still wear more jeans than anyone else.

A conjunctive adverb or transitional expression may move around within its clause, so the semicolon will not always come just before the adverb or expression. The adverb or expression itself is usually set off with a comma or commas.

Blue jeans have become fashionable all over the world**;** the American originators**,** *however,* still wear more jeans than anyone else.

22c. Semicolons with series

Between series items

Use semicolons (rather than commas) to separate items in a series when the items contain commas.

The custody case involved Amy Dalton, the child**;** Ellen and Mark Dalton, the parents**;** and Ruth and Hal Blum, the grandparents.

Not before a series

Do not use a semicolon to introduce a series. (Use a colon or a dash instead.)

Not	Teachers have heard all sorts of reasons why students do poorly; psychological problems, family illness, too much work, too little time.
But	Teachers have heard all sorts of reasons why students do poorly: psychological problems, family illness, too much work, too little time.

23
THE COLON

The colon is mainly a mark of introduction, but it has a few other conventional uses as well.

23a. Colon for introduction

At end of main clause

The colon ends a complete sentence (main clause°) and introduces various additions:

Soul food has a deceptively simple definition: the ethnic cooking of African-Americans. [Introduces an explanation.]

At least three soul food dishes are familiar to most Americans: fried chicken, barbecued spareribs, and sweet potatoes. [Introduces a series.]

Soul food has one disadvantage: fat. [Introduces an appositive.°]

One soul food chef has a solution: "Instead of using ham hocks to flavor beans, I use smoked turkey wings. The soulful, smoky taste remains, but without all the fat of pork." [Introduces a long quotation.]

Not inside main clause

Do not use a colon inside a main clause, especially after *such as* or a verb.

Not	The best-known soul food dish is: fried chicken. Many Americans have not tasted delicacies such as: chitlins and black-eyed peas.
But	The best-known soul food dish is fried chicken. Many Americans have not tasted delicacies such as chitlins and black-eyed peas.

23b. Colon with salutations of business letters, titles and subtitles, divisions of time, and biblical citations

Salutation of a business letter
Dear Ms. Burak**:**

Title and subtitle
*Anna Freud***:** *Her Life and Work*

Time		**Biblical citation**
12:26	6:00	1 Corinthians 3:6–7

24
THE APOSTROPHE

The apostrophe (') appears as part of a word to indicate possession, the omission of one or more letters, or (in a few cases) plural number.

24a. Apostrophe with possessives

The POSSESSIVE form of a word indicates that it owns or is the source of another word: *the dog's hair, everyone's hope.* For nouns° and indefinite pronouns,° such as *everyone,* the possessive form always includes an apostrophe and often an *-s.*

NOTE The apostrophe or apostrophe-plus-*s* is an *addition.* Before this addition, always spell the name of the owner or owners without dropping or adding letters.

Singular words: Add -*'s.*

Bill *Boughton's* skillful card tricks amaze children.
Anyone's eyes would widen.

The -*'s* ending for singular words pertains to singular words ending in -*s.*

Sandra *Cisneros's* work is highly regarded.
The *business's* customers filed suit.

Plural words ending in -*s:* Add -*'* only.

Workers' incomes have fallen slightly over the past year.
Many students take several *years'* leave after high school.
The *Murphys'* son lives at home.

Plural words not ending in -*s:* Add -'*s.*

Children's educations are at stake.
We need to attract the *media's* attention.

Compound words: Add -'*s* only to the last word.

The *brother-in-law's* business failed.
Taxes are always *somebody else's* fault.

Two or more owners: Add -'*s* depending on possession.

Youngman's and *Mason's* comedy techniques are similar.
[Each comedian has his own technique.]

The child recovered despite her *mother and father's* ne-
glect. [The mother and father were jointly neglectful.]

24b. Misuses of the apostrophe

Not with plural nouns°

Not   The unleashed *dog's* belonged to the *Jones'.*

But   The unleashed *dogs* belonged to the *Joneses.*

Not with singular verbs°

Not   The subway *break's* down less often now.

But   The subway *breaks* down less often now.

Not with possessives of personal pronouns°

Not   The car is *her's,* not *their's.* *It's* color is red.

But   The car is *hers,* not *theirs.* *Its* color is red.

Note Don't confuse possessive pronouns and contractions: *its, your, their,* and *whose* are possessives. *It's,
you're, they're,* and *who's* are contractions. See below.

24c. Apostrophe with contractions

A CONTRACTION replaces one or more letters, numbers,
or words with an apostrophe.

it is	it's	cannot	can't
you are	you're	does not	doesn't
they are	they're	were not	weren't
who is	who's	class of 1997	class of '97

Note Don't misuse the four contractions on the left for
the possessive pronouns° *its, your, their,* and *whose.*

24c

24d. Apostrophe with plural letters, numbers, and words named as words

You may cite a character or word as a word rather than use it for its meaning. When such an element is plural, add an apostrophe plus *-s*.

This sentence has too many <u>but</u>'s.
Remember to dot your <u>i</u>'s and cross your <u>t</u>'s.
At the end of each poem, the author had written two <u>3</u>'s.

Notice that the cited element is underlined (italicized) but the apostrophe and added *-s* are not.

25

QUOTATION MARKS

Quotation marks—either double (" ") or single (' ')—mainly enclose direct quotations from speech and from writing.

This chapter treats the main uses of quotation marks. For when to use quotations from sources in a paper, see pages 97–98. For how to integrate quotations into your own prose, see pages 101–02. For punctuation to use when altering quotations, see pages 67–69.

NOTE Quotation marks *always* come in pairs, one before and one after the quoted material.

25a. Quotation marks with direct quotations

Double quotation marks

A DIRECT QUOTATION reports what someone said or wrote, in the exact words of the original.

"Life," said the psychoanalyst Karen Horney, "remains a very efficient therapist."

NOTE Do not use quotation marks with an INDIRECT QUOTATION, which reports what someone said or wrote but not in the exact words of the original.

Single quotation marks

Use single quotation marks to enclose a quotation within a quotation.

"In formulating any philosophy," Woody Allen writes, "the first consideration must always be: What can we know? . . .

Descartes hinted at the problem when he wrote, **'**My mind can never know my body, although it has become quite friendly with my leg.**'** "

Long quotations

Use an indention to set off long quotations from the main body of your text. *Do not use quotation marks with a set-off quotation.*

In his 1967 study of the lives of unemployed

black men, Elliot Liebow observes that "un-

skilled" construction work requires more expe-

rience and skill than is generally assumed.

> A healthy, sturdy, active man of good
>
> intelligence requires from two to
>
> four weeks to break in on a construc-
>
> tion job. . . . It frequently happens
>
> that his foreman or the craftsman he
>
> services is not willing to wait that
>
> long for him to get into condition or
>
> to learn at a glance the difference
>
> in size between a rough 2 x 8 and a
>
> finished 2 x 10. (62)

(The parenthetical number at the end of the quotation is a source citation.)

The length of a set-off quotation and method of displaying it vary among academic disciplines. Here are the formats recommended by the principal discipline guides:

English, foreign languages, and some other humanities (*MLA Handbook for Writers of Research Papers,* 4th ed.): This is the style illustrated above. Set off four or more lines of poetry and five or more typed lines of prose. Indent the quotation one inch or ten spaces from the left, double-space the quotation, and double-space above and below the quotation.

History, art history, and some other humanities (*The Chicago Manual of Style,* 14th ed., and the student guide adapted from it, Kate L. Turabian's *A Manual for Writers of Term Papers, Theses, and Dissertations,* 6th ed.): Set off poetry of more than two lines. Set off prose of more than four to ten lines, depending on your reason for quoting and the number of displayed quotations you have. (For instance, you might set off a number of shorter quotations when you are comparing them.) Indent any displayed quotation five spaces from the left, single-space the quotation, and double-space above and below it.

Psychology and some other disciplines (*Publication Manual of the American Psychological Association,* 4th ed.): Set off quotations of forty or more words. For student papers, indent the quotation five spaces from the left, single-space the quotation, and double-space above and below the quotation.

Life sciences, physical sciences, and mathematics (*Scientific Style and Format: The CBE Manual for Authors, Editors, and Publishers,* 6th ed.): This guide specifies only that long quotations be set off and indented, so any of the formats above is appropriate.

Dialog

When quoting a conversation, put the speeches in double quotation marks and begin a new paragraph for each speaker.

> "What shall I call you? Your name?" Andrews whispered rapidly, as with a high squeak the latch of the door rose.
> "Elizabeth," she said. "Elizabeth."
>
> —GRAHAM GREENE, *The Man Within*

25b. Quotation marks with titles of works

Within your text use quotation marks to enclose the titles of works that are published or released within larger works (see below). Use underlining (italics) for all other titles (see p. 88).

SONG
"Satisfaction"

SHORT STORY
"The Gift of the Magi"

SHORT POEM
"Her Kind"

ARTICLE IN A PERIODICAL
"Does 'Scaring' Work?"

ESSAY
"Joey: A 'Mechanical Boy' "

EPISODE OF A TELEVISION OR RADIO PROGRAM
"The Mexican Connection" (on <u>60 Minutes</u>)

SUBDIVISION OF A BOOK
"The Mast Head" (Chapter 35 of <u>Moby Dick</u>)

NOTE Some academic disciplines do not require quotation marks for titles within source citations. See pages 128–34 (APA style) and 135–38 (CBE style).

25c. Quotation marks with defined words

By "charity" I mean the love of one's neighbor as oneself.

NOTE Underlining (italics) may also highlight defined words. (See p. 89.)

25d. Quotation marks with other punctuation

Commas and periods: inside quotation marks

25d

Jonathan Swift wrote a famous satire, "A Modest Proposal," in 1729.

"Swift's 'A Modest Proposal,'" wrote one critic, "is so outrageous that it cannot be believed."

Colons and semicolons: outside quotation marks

A few years ago the slogan in elementary education was "learning by playing"; now educators focus on basic skills.

We all know the meaning of "basic skills": reading, writing, and arithmetic.

Dashes, question marks, and exclamation points: inside quotation marks only if part of the quotation

When a dash, question mark, or exclamation point is part of the quotation, place it *inside* quotation marks. Don't use any other punctuation, such as a period or comma.

"But must you—" Marcia hesitated, afraid of the answer.
The stranger asked, "Where am I?"
"Go away!" I yelled.

When a dash, question mark, or exclamation point applies only to the larger sentence, not to the quotation, place it *outside* quotation marks—again, with no other punctuation.

Betty Friedan's question in 1963—"Who knows what women can be?"—encouraged generations of women to seek answers.

Who said, "Now cracks a noble heart"?

The woman called me "stupid"!

When both the quotation and the larger sentence take a question mark or exclamation point, use only the one *inside* the quotation mark.

Did you say, "Who is she?"

26
OTHER MARKS

The other marks of punctuation are the dash, parentheses, the ellipsis mark, brackets, and the slash.

26a. Dash or dashes for shifts and interruptions

The dash (–) punctuates sentences. In contrast, the hyphen (-) punctuates words. Form a dash with two hyphens (--). Do not add extra space before, after, or between the hyphens.

Shifts in tone or thought

The novel—if one could call it that—appeared in 1994.

If the book had a plot—but a plot would be too conventional.

Nonessential elements

You may use dashes instead of commas to set off and emphasize elements that are not essential to the meaning of your sentence (see p. 54). Be sure to use a pair of dashes when the element interrupts the sentence.

The qualities Monet painted—sunlight, rich shadows, deep colors—abounded near the rivers and gardens he used as subjects.

Introductory series and concluding series and explanations

Shortness of breath, skin discoloration, persistent indigestion, the presence of small lumps—all these may signify cancer. [Introductory series.]

The patient undergoes a battery of tests—CAT scan, bronchoscopy, perhaps even biopsy. [Concluding series.]

Many patients are disturbed by the CAT scan—by the need to keep still for long periods in an exceedingly small space. [Concluding explanation.]

You may use a colon (p. 59) instead of a dash in the last two examples. The dash is more informal.

26b. Parentheses for nonessential elements

Parentheses always come in pairs, one before and one after the punctuated material.

Parenthetical expressions

Parentheses de-emphasize PARENTHETICAL EXPRESSIONS —explanatory, supplemental, or transitional words or phrases. (Commas emphasize these expressions more and dashes still more.)

The population of Philadelphia (now about 1.6 million) has declined since 1950.

Don't put a comma before a parenthetical expression enclosed in parentheses. Punctuation after the parenthetical expression should be placed outside the closing parenthesis.

NOT Philadelphia's population compares with Houston's, (about 1.6 million.)

BUT Philadelphia's population compares with Houston's (about 1.6 million).

Labels for lists

Philadelphia's chief manufacturing industries are (1) chemicals, (2) pharmaceuticals, (3) medical devices, and (4) transportation equipment.

26c. Ellipsis mark for omissions from quotations

The ellipsis mark consists of three spaced periods (. . .). It generally indicates an omission from a quotation, as illustrated in the following excerpts from this quotation about the Philippines:

ORIGINAL QUOTATION

"It was the Cuba of the future. It was going the way of Iran. It was another Nicaragua, another Cambodia, another Vietnam. But all these places, awesome in their histories, are so different from each other that one couldn't help thinking: this kind of talk was a shorthand for a confusion. All that was being said was that something was happening in the Philippines. Or more plausibly, a lot of different

things were happening in the Philippines. And a lot of people were feeling obliged to speak out about it."

—JAMES FENTON, "The Philippine Election"

OMISSION OF THE MIDDLE OF A SENTENCE

"But all these places . . . are so different from each other
that one couldn't help thinking: this kind of talk was a
shorthand for a confusion."

OMISSION OF THE END OF A SENTENCE

"It was another Nicaragua. . . ." [The sentence period,
closed up to the last word, precedes the ellipsis mark.]

"It was another Nicaragua . . ." (Fenton 25). [When the
quotation is followed by a parenthetical source citation,
as here, the sentence period follows the citation.]

OMISSION OF PARTS OF TWO SENTENCES

"All that was being said was that . . . a lot of different
things were happening in the Philippines."

OMISSION OF ONE OR MORE SENTENCES

"It was the Cuba of the future. It was going the way of
Iran. It was another Nicaragua, another Cambodia, another Vietnam. . . . All that was being said was that something was happening in the Philippines."

Note these features of the examples:

- The ellipsis mark indicates that material is omitted
from the source when the omission would not otherwise be clear. Thus, use an ellipsis mark when the
words you quote form a complete sentence that is different in the original (first through fourth examples).
Don't use an ellipsis mark at the beginning or end of a
partial sentence: *Fenton calls the Philippines "another
Nicaragua."*
- After a grammatically complete sentence, an ellipsis
mark usually follows a sentence period and a space
(second and last examples). The exception occurs
when a parenthetical source citation follows the quotation (third example), in which case the sentence period
falls after the citation.

If you omit one or more lines of poetry or paragraphs
of prose from a quotation, use a separate line of ellipsis
marks across the full width of the quotation to show the
omission.

26d. Brackets for changes in quotations

Brackets have highly specialized uses in mathematical equations, but their main use for all kinds of writing is to indicate that you have altered a quotation to explain, clarify, or correct it.

"That Texaco station [just outside Chicago] is one of the busiest in the nation," said a company spokesperson.

26e. Slash for options and between lines of poetry

Option

Some teachers oppose pass/fail courses.

Between lines of poetry

When you run two lines of poetry into your text, separate them with a slash surrounded by space.

Many readers have sensed a reluctant turn away from death in Frost's lines "The woods are lovely, dark and deep, / But I have promises to keep."

IV

CONVENTIONS OF FORM AND APPEARANCE

27. Document Format *71*

28. The Hyphen *85*

29. Capital Letters *86*

30. Underlining (Italics) *88*

31. Abbreviations *90*

32. Numbers *92*

27
DOCUMENT FORMAT

Legible, consistent, and attractive papers and correspondence serve your readers and reflect well on you. This chapter shows the basics of formatting any document clearly and effectively (27a), provides design guidelines for academic papers in various disciplines (27b), and discusses formats for business correspondence such as job-application letters, résumés, and electronic mail (27c).

27a. Clear and effective documents

Your papers, reports, and correspondence must of course be neat and legible. That means, at a minimum, a readable typeface, adequate margins, and very few, if any, corrections. But you can do more to make your work accessible and attractive, especially if you work on a computerized word processor. You can use paper, type, white space, headings, lists, and illustrations to put your ideas across efficiently and forcefully.

27a

Paper

Unless your project demands otherwise, use $8\frac{1}{2}'' \times 11''$ white bond paper of at least sixteen-pound weight, and use the same type of paper throughout a project. Type or print on only one side of each sheet. If your printer uses fanfold paper, remove the rows of holes along the sides and separate the pages at the folds before submitting the final document.

Type

PRINT QUALITY

Type or print all documents. (Handwriting may be acceptable in some academic assignments, but always check with your instructor before submitting a handwritten paper.) Use black type, making sure that the typewriter's or printer's ribbon or cartridge is fresh enough to produce a dark impression. If you use a dot-matrix printer (which forms characters out of tiny dots), make sure the tails on letters such as *j*, *p*, and *y* fall below the line of type, as they do here.

TEXT

Academic papers are generally double-spaced; busi-

71

ness writing is often single-spaced. See pages 77–81 and 81–84, respectively, for more on the spacing of lines.

The type for the text of your document should be at least 10 or 12 points, as illustrated by these type samples:

12-point Courier 12-point Times Roman

10-point Courier 10-point Times Roman

Use one space between words and after most punctuation, including the punctuation at the ends of sentences. (For the special spacing with ellipsis marks, which show omissions from quotations, see pp. 67–68.) Type a dash with two hyphens (--). Use handwriting to make symbols that are not on your keyboard.

Within the text use <u>underlining</u>, *italics*, or **boldface** to emphasize key words or sentences. (See Chapter 30.) For academic research writing, ask your instructor whether he or she prefers underlining or italics with source citations. Note that many readers consider the constant use of type embellishments to be distracting. Vary type selectively to enhance your meaning, not just to decorate your work.

27a

LONG QUOTATIONS

Set off long quotations according to the guidelines for various disciplines on pages 63–64.

SOURCE CITATIONS

If you need to cite sources for your work, follow one of the systems discussed on pages 104–38, as appropriate for the field you're writing in.

CORRECTIONS

Business correspondence should be error-free, without visible corrections. Academic writing permits some corrections. Make your corrections *neatly*, either on a typewriter or by hand in black ink. If a page has more than a few errors, retype or reprint it.

White space, headings, and lists

The white space on a page eases crowding, highlights elements, and focuses readers' attention.

PARAGRAPH BREAKS

An indention at the beginning of a paragraph (in double-spaced copy) or extra space between paragraphs (in single-spaced copy) gives readers a break and reassures them that you have divided ideas into manageable chunks.

MARGINS

Use minimum one-inch margins on all sides of every page. Use a larger left margin if you plan to bind the document on the left. An uneven right margin is almost always acceptable. If your word processor or typewriter will produce an even (or justified) right margin, use the feature only if it does not sometimes leave wide spaces between words.

HEADINGS

In a research paper, business report, or similarly long and complex document, headings within the text can clarify organization and the relationships among parts. When you use headings, follow these guidelines:

- Create an outline of your document in order to plan where headings should go. Inconsistent, overlapping, or missing headings do more harm than good.
- Keep headings as short as possible while making them specific about the material that follows.
- Word headings consistently—for instance, all questions (*What Is the Scientific Method?*), all phrases° with *-ing* words (*Understanding the Scientific Method*), or all phrases with nouns (*The Scientific Method*).
- Indicate the relative importance of headings with type size, positioning, and highlighting, such as capital letters and underlining.

27a

```
          FIRST-LEVEL HEADING
```

Second-Level Heading

```
Third-Level Heading
```

A word processor provides more type styles and sizes than most typewriters.

FIRST-LEVEL HEADING

Second-Level Heading

Third-Level Heading

- Keep the appearance simple: most reports or papers shouldn't need more than two type styles or two or three type sizes (including the body type). Avoid extra-large letters and unusual styles of type (such as outline and shadow type).
- Don't break a page immediately after a heading. Push the heading to the next page.

NOTE Document format in psychology and some other social sciences requires a particular treatment of headings. See page 80.

LISTS

Whenever your document contains a list of related items—for example, the steps in a process or the elements in a proposal—consider setting the items off and marking them with numbers or bullets (centered dots, used in the list below about tables and illustrations). A list is easier to read than a paragraph and adds white space to the page. Most word-processing programs can format a numbered or bulleted list automatically.

Tables and illustrations

Tables and illustrations (graphs, charts, diagrams, photographs) can often make a point for you more efficiently and effectively than words can. Tables and illustrations present data, make comparisons, explain processes, show changes, and represent what something looks like, among other uses. Whatever kind of table or illustration you plan, follow these guidelines:

27a

- Focus on a purpose for the table or illustration—a single point you want it to make. Otherwise, it may be too complex and may confuse readers.
- Provide a title for the table or illustration so that the reader knows immediately what its purpose and content are. Generally, a table's title falls above the table, whereas an illustration's title falls below.
- Make the table or illustration legible and attractive.
- Provide clear labels for all parts, such as columns and rows in a table, bars in a graph, and parts of a machine in a drawing. In the interest of clarity, avoid abbreviations unless you know your readers will understand them.
- Provide a source note whenever the data or the entire table or illustration is someone else's independent material (see p. 98). Each discipline has a slightly different style for such source notes; those in the table opposite and the figures on page 76 reflect the style of the social sciences. See also Chapters 38–41.
- Number tables and figures separately (Table 1, Table 2, etc.; Figure 1, Figure 2, etc.).
- Refer to each table or figure (for instance, "See Figure 2") at the point(s) in the text where readers will benefit by consulting it.

- Unless your document includes many tables and/or illustrations, place each one on a page by itself immediately after the page that refers to it.

Many organizations and academic disciplines have preferred styles for tables and figures that may differ from those presented here. When in doubt about how to prepare and place tables and illustrations, ask your instructor or supervisor.

TABLES

Tables usually summarize raw data, displaying the data concisely and clearly.

Table 1

Incidence of Courtship Violence

Type of violence	Number of students reporting	Percentage of sample
Insulted or swore	62	50.4
Threatened to hit or throw something	17	13.8
Threw something	8	6.5
Pushed, grabbed, or shoved	18	14.6
Slapped	8	6.6
Kicked, bit, or hit with fist	7	5.7
Hit or tried to hit with something	2	1.6
Threatened with a knife or gun	1	0.8
Used a knife or gun	1	0.8

Note. Data from "Recent Increases in Dating Violence," by M. Laner, 1983, Social Problems, 22, p. 160.

ILLUSTRATIONS

Illustrations often recast data into visual form. Pie charts, bar graphs, and line graphs are helpful for comparisons, such as changes and proportions.

27a

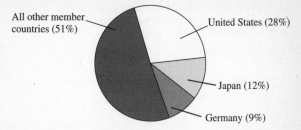

Figure 1. Member countries' assessments to United Nations budget of $1.1 billion in 1994. From "The U.N. at 50," by R. Mylan, 1995, October 18, *Newsweek*, p. 17.

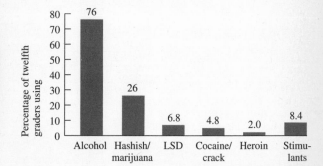

Figure 2. Use of alcohol, compared to other drugs, among twelfth graders (1993). Data from *Monitoring the Future Study*, 1994, Ann Arbor, MI: University of Michigan Press.

Figure 3. Five-year cumulative return for equities in Standard & Poor's 500 Index, 1990–1994.

NOTE Graphics software and some word-processing software will create tables, graphs, charts, and other illustrations when you supply the raw data. If you use many tables and illustrations in your writing, you'll find it worthwhile to master computerized graphics.

27b. Academic papers

The principles of document format discussed in section 27a apply generally to academic writing, but most disciplines require specific variations to suit the needs of their research and writing.

English, foreign languages, and some other humanities: MLA format

The style guide for English and some other humanities is the *MLA Handbook for Writers of Research Papers*, 4th edition (1995), published by the Modern Language Association. This guide recommends a document format like the one discussed in section 27a for paper, type, margins, and illustrations. The samples below show details of this format.

Number all pages, starting with 1 for the first page and continuing in sequence through any endnotes and the list of works cited. Add your last name just before each page number, as illustrated by "Perez" in the samples.

FIRST PAGE OF PAPER

Perez 1

Terry Perez

Professor Christensen

English 100

November 16, 1995

America's Media Image ◄── Center

Is the United States a monoculture, a unified, homogeneous society? Many Americans think that it is or should be. But the writer

---

½"
Perez 2

Everyone complains that the media never pre-

1"   sent enough good news. When it comes to eth-   1"

nic relations, this is certainly the case.

~~~~~~

the older women on <u>Golden Girls</u>, and more re-

1"   cent African-American situation comedies and   1"

dramas. However, the norm is easy to see.

1"

NOTE For MLA style for long quotations set off from the text, see page 63. For MLA style for source citations, see pages 104–18.

27b

History, art history, philosophy, and some other humanities: *Chicago Manual* format

The Chicago Manual of Style, 14th edition (1993), serves as a style guide for history, art history, philosophy, and some other humanities. A guide for students adapted from *The Chicago Manual* is Kate L. Turabian, *A Manual for Writers of Term Papers, Theses, and Dissertations*, 6th edition, revised by John Grossman and Alice Bennett (1996). The document format discussed in section 27a resembles those recommended by both of these books. For spacing and arranging elements, use the MLA format illustrated above, with the following exceptions:

- Number pages with a number only, consecutively from the first page through the entire paper. On the first page of the paper and the first page of any endnotes and the bibliography, place the page number at the bottom of the page, centered. On all other pages, place the number at the top, either centered or at the right margin, and double-space to the text below.
- Capitalize the title, and triple-space beneath it.
- *A Manual for Writers* suggests a separate title page, table of contents, and other preliminary elements for long, multichapter works. Consult the guide if your project or your instructor requires such elements.

NOTE See page 63 for *Chicago Manual* and *Manual for Writers* style for long quotations set off from the text. And see pages 118–25 for these books' style for source citations.

Psychology and some other social sciences: APA format

The style guide for psychology, educational psychology, and some other social sciences is the *Publication Manual of the American Psychological Association,* 4th edition (1994). APA document format for student papers corresponds closely to the guidelines in section 27a, with some exceptions shown on the following samples.

TITLE PAGE

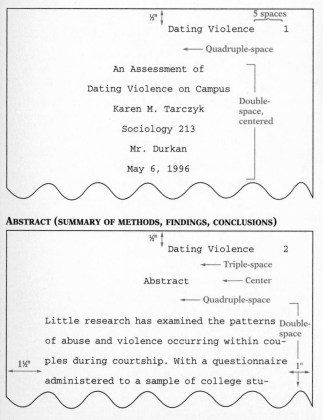

ABSTRACT (SUMMARY OF METHODS, FINDINGS, CONCLUSIONS)

27b

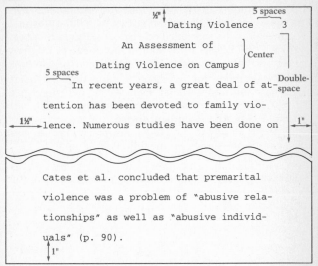

Number the pages consecutively, beginning with 1 for the title page and continuing through any endnotes and the references. Before each page number, provide a shortened version of your title ("Dating Violence" in the samples). Separate the shortened title and page number with five spaces.

For headings in social science papers, use these formats, always double-spacing:

First-Level Heading

Second-Level Heading

  Third-level heading. Run this heading into
the text paragraph.

NOTE See page 64 for the APA style for long quotations set off from the text. And see pages 125–34 for APA style for source citations.

Life sciences, physical sciences, and mathematics: CBE style

The style guide for the life sciences and often for the physical sciences and mathematics is *Scientific Style and Format: The CBE Manual for Authors, Editors, and Publishers,* 6th edition (1994), published for the Council of

Biology Editors. For student papers (as opposed to those planned for publication), use a format like that shown for APA style (pp. 79–80), including title page and abstract. (You may omit the shortened title before the page number.)

Note For CBE style for long quotations set off from the text, see page 64. For CBE style for source citations, see pages 134–38.

27c. Business correspondence

The essential document format discussed in section 27a applies to most business writing, with important additions for headings and other elements. This section discusses the business letter, using the example of the job-application letter, and the résumé. It also briefly discusses electronic mail, which has a format of its own.

Job-application letter

In any letter to a businessperson, you are addressing someone who wants to see quickly why you are writing and how to respond to you. For a job application, announce right off what job you are applying for and how you heard about it. (See the sample letter on the next page.) Summarize your qualifications for the job, including facts about your education and employment history that qualify you for the job. Don't recite what's on the résumé; instead, highlight and reshape the relevant parts of the résumé for the particular job. At the end of the letter, mention when you are available for an interview and provide your phone number.

27c

For any business correspondence, use either unlined white paper measuring 8½" × 11" or what is called letterhead stationery with your address printed at the top of the sheet. Type the letter single-spaced (with double space between elements) on only one side of a sheet, following the model on the next page.

For the salutation, which greets the addressee, use a job title (*Dear Personnel Manager*) or use a general salutation (*Dear Sir or Madam*)—unless of course you know the addressee's name. When addressing a woman by name, use *Ms.* when she has no other title, when you don't know how she prefers to be addressed, or when you know she prefers *Ms.* For the letter's close, choose an expression that reflects the formality in the salutation: *Respectfully, Cordially, Yours truly,* and *Sincerely* are more formal than *Regards* and *Best wishes.*

27c

3712 Swiss Avenue
Dallas, TX 75204
March 4, 1996

Personnel Manager
Dallas News
Communications Center
Dallas, TX 75222

Dear Personnel Manager:

In response to your posting in the English
Department of Southern Methodist University, I am applying for the summer job of
part-time editorial assistant for the
Dallas News.

I am now enrolled at Southern Methodist
University as a sophomore, with a dual
major in English literature and journalism. My courses so far have included news
reporting, copy editing, and electronic
publishing. I worked a summer as a copy
aide for my hometown newspaper, and for
two years I have edited and written sports
stories and features for the university
newspaper. My feature articles cover subjects as diverse as campus elections,
parking regulations, visiting professors,
and speech codes.

As the enclosed résumé and writing samples
indicate, my education and practical knowledge of newspaper work prepare me for the
opening you have.

I am available for an interview at your
convenience and would be happy to show
more samples of my writing. Please call me
at 744-3816.

Sincerely,

Ian M. Irvine
Ian M. Irvine

Enc.

The envelope should show your name and address in the upper-left corner and the addressee's name, title, and address in the center. Use an envelope that will accommodate the letter once it is folded horizontally in thirds.

Résumé

The résumé that you enclose with a letter of application should contain, in table form, your name and address, career objective, and education and employment histories, along with information about how to obtain your references. (See the sample on the next page.) Use headings to mark the various sections of the résumé, spacing around them and within sections so that important information stands out. Try to limit your résumé to one page so that it can be quickly scanned. However, if your experience and education are extensive, a two-page résumé is preferable to a single cramped, unreadable page.

In preparing your résumé, you may wish to consult one of the many books devoted to application letters, résumés, and other elements of a job search. Two helpful guides are Richard N. Bolles, *What Color Is Your Parachute? A Practical Manual for Job-Hunters and Career Changers,* and Tom Jackson, *The Perfect Résumé.*

27c

Electronic mail

Electronic mail (E-mail) sent over computer networks is usually more informal and often more terse than other business correspondence. Generally, the headings in an E-mail message are dictated by the network, but you can still address your reader(s) by name and sign off with your own name. Within the message, use conventional paragraphing and white space between paragraphs to increase readability. In a long message, consider using headings to break up the text and direct your readers' attention.

Electronic mail rarely allows underlining, italics, or boldface, so you can't emphasize or highlight words conventionally. E-mail writers have devised some substitutes, including asterisks before and after the words to be highlighted (*I *will not* be able to attend the meeting*) or an underscore before and after a book title (*The book is _Public Relations_*). Avoid using all-capital letters for emphasis: they yell too loud. An E-mail message entirely in capital letters may be considered rude, no matter what its content.

Ian M. Irvine
3712 Swiss Avenue
Dallas, Texas 75204
Telephone: 214-744-3816

Position desired
Part-time editorial assistant.

Education
Southern Methodist University, 1994 to present.
Current standing: sophomore.
Major: English literature and journalism.
Journalism courses: news reporting, copy edit-
ing, electronic publishing, communications
arts, broadcast journalism.

Abilene (Texas) Senior High School, 1990-1994.
Graduated with academic, college-preparatory
degree.

Employment history
1994 to present. Reporter, Daily Campus, student newspaper of Southern Methodist
University.
Write regular coverage of baseball, track, and
soccer teams. Write feature stories on campus
policies and events. Edit sports news, campus
listings, features.

Summer 1995. Copy aide, Abilene Reporter-News.
Routed copy, monitored teleprinter, ran
errands, and assisted reporters with research.

Summer 1994. Painter, Longhorn Painters,
Abilene.
Prepared and painted exteriors and interiors
of houses.

References
Academic: Placement Office
               Southern Methodist University
               Dallas, TX 75275

Employment: Ms. Millie Stevens
               Abilene Reporter-News
               Abilene, TX 79604

Personal: Ms. Sheryl Gipstein
               26 Overland Drive
               Abilene, TX 79604

Always use a hyphen to divide a word between sylla-bles from one line to the next. Also use it to form some COMPOUND WORDS, such as *cross-reference,* that express a combination of ideas. The following rules cover many but not all compounds. When you doubt the spelling of a compound word, consult a dictionary.

28a. Compound adjectives

When two or more words serve together as a single modifier° before a noun, a hyphen forms the modifying words clearly into a unit.

> She is a *well-known* actor.
> No *English-speaking* people were in the room.

When such a compound modifier follows the noun, the hyphen is unnecessary.

> The actor is *well known.*
> Those people are *English speaking.*

The hyphen is also unnecessary in a compound modifier containing an *-ly* adverb, even before the noun: *clearly de-fined terms.*

28b. Fractions and compound numbers

Hyphens join the parts of fractions: *three-fourths, one-half.* And the whole numbers *twenty-one* to *ninety-nine* are always hyphenated.

28c. Prefixes and suffixes

Prefixes are usually attached to word stems without hyphens: *predetermine, unnatural, disengage.* However, a hyphen usually separates the two when the prefix pre-cedes a capitalized word, when a capital letter is com-bined with a word, or when the combination links two of the same vowel or three of the same consonant in a way that could cause misreading: *un-American, A-frame, de-emphasize, trill-like.* And some prefixes, such as *self-, all-,* and *ex-* (meaning "formerly"), usually require hy-phens no matter what follows: *self-control, all-inclusive, ex-student.* The only suffix that regularly requires a hy-phen is *-elect,* as in *president-elect.*

CAPITAL LETTERS

The following conventions and a desk dictionary can help you decide whether to capitalize a particular word. In general, capitalize only when a rule or the dictionary says you must.

NOTE The social, natural, and applied sciences require specialized capitalization for terminology, such as *Conditions A and B* or *Escherichia coli*. Consult one of the style guides listed on pages 103–04 for the requirements of the discipline you are writing in.

29a. First word of a sentence

Every writer should own a good dictionary.

29b. Proper nouns and adjectives

PROPER NOUNS name specific persons, places, and things: *Shakespeare, California, World War I*. PROPER ADJECTIVES are formed from some proper nouns: *Shakespearean, Californian*. Capitalize all proper nouns and proper adjectives but not the articles (*a, an, the*) that precede them.

SPECIFIC PERSONS AND THINGS

Stephen King	Boulder Dam

SPECIFIC PLACES AND GEOGRAPHICAL REGIONS

New York City	the Northeast, the South

But: northeast of the city, going south

DAYS OF THE WEEK, MONTHS, HOLIDAYS

Monday	Yom Kippur
May	Christmas

HISTORICAL EVENTS, DOCUMENTS, PERIODS, MOVEMENTS

the Vietnam War	the Renaissance
the Constitution	the Romantic Movement

GOVERNMENT OFFICES OR DEPARTMENTS AND INSTITUTIONS

House of Representatives	Polk Municipal Court
Department of Defense	Northeast High School

POLITICAL, SOCIAL, ATHLETIC, AND OTHER ORGANIZATIONS AND THEIR MEMBERS

B'nai B'rith	Democratic Party, Democrats
Rotary Club	Atlanta Falcons
League of Women Voters	Chicago Symphony Orchestra

RACES, NATIONALITIES, AND THEIR LANGUAGES

Native American	Germans
African-American, Negro	Swahili
Caucasian	Italian

But: blacks, whites

RELIGIONS, THEIR FOLLOWERS, AND TERMS FOR THE SACRED

Christianity, Christians	God
Catholicism, Catholics	Allah
Judaism, Orthodox Jew	the Bible (*but* biblical)
Islam, Moslems *or* Muslims	the Koran

COMMON NOUNS AS PARTS OF PROPER NOUNS

Main Street	Lake Superior
Ventura Avenue	Ford Motor Company
Central Park	Madison College
Mississippi River	King's County
Pacific Ocean	George Washington Memorial

But: the ocean, college course, the company

29c. Titles and subtitles of works

Within your text, capitalize all the words in a title and subtitle *except* the following: articles (*a, an, the*), *to* in infinitives,° and connecting words (prepositions° and conjunctions°) of fewer than five letters. Capitalize even these short words when they are the first or last word in a title or when they fall after a colon or semicolon.

"Once More to the Lake"	*Management: A New Theory*
A Diamond Is Forever	"Courtship Through the Ages"
"Knowing Whom to Ask"	*File Under Architecture*
Learning from Las Vegas	*An End to Live For*

NOTE Some academic disciplines require a different treatment of titles within source citations, such as capitalizing only the first words of some or all titles. See pages 128–34 (APA style) and 135–38 (CBE style).

29d. Titles of persons

Before a person's name, capitalize his or her title. After the name, do not capitalize the title.

Professor Otto Osborne   Otto Osborne, a professor
Doctor Jane Covington   Jane Covington, a doctor
Senator Jesse Helms   Jesse Helms, the senator

30

UNDERLINING (ITALICS)

Underlining and *italic type* indicate the same thing: the word or words are being distinguished or emphasized. In business the almost universal use of computerized word processors makes both forms of highlighting possible, and italics may be preferred. In schools the use of italics is less common, and many disciplines continue to require underlining for works in source citations. Consult your instructor before you use italic type.

NOTE If you underline two or more words in a row, underline the space between the words, too: Criminal Statistics: Misuses of Numbers.

30a. Titles of works

Within your text, underline the titles of works, such as books and periodicals, that are published, released, or produced separately from other works. (See below.) Use quotation marks for all other titles, such as short stories and articles in periodicals. (See p. 64.)

BOOK
War and Peace

PLAY
Hamlet

PAMPHLET
The Truth About
    Alcoholism

LONG MUSICAL WORK
The Beatles' Revolver
But: Symphony in C

LONG POEM
Paradise Lost

PERIODICAL
Philadelphia Inquirer

PUBLISHED SPEECH
Lincoln's Gettysburg
    Address

TELEVISION OR RADIO PROGRAM
60 Minutes

WORK OF VISUAL ART	**MOVIE**
Michelangelo's <u>David</u>	<u>Psycho</u>

EXCEPTIONS Legal documents, the Bible, and their parts are generally not underlined.

NOT   We studied the <u>Book of Revelation</u> in the New English <u>Bible</u>.

BUT   We studied the Book of Revelation in the New English Bible.

NOTE Some academic disciplines do not require underlining or italics for some or all titles within source citations. See pages 128–34 (APA style) and 135–38 (CBE style).

30b. Ships, aircraft, spacecraft, trains

<u>Challenger</u>	<u>Orient Express</u>	<u>Queen Elizabeth 2</u>
<u>Apollo XI</u>	<u>Montrealer</u>	<u>Spirit of St. Louis</u>

30d

30c. Foreign words

Underline a foreign expression that has not been absorbed into our language. A dictionary will say whether a word is still considered foreign to English.

The scientific name for the brown trout is <u>Salmo trutta</u>. [The Latin scientific names for plants and animals are always underlined.]

The Latin <u>De gustibus non est disputandum</u> translates roughly as "There's no accounting for taste."

30d. Words, letters, and numbers named as words

Underline characters or words that are cited as words rather than used for their meanings.

Some people pronounce <u>th</u>, as in <u>thought</u>, with a faint <u>s</u> or <u>f</u> sound.

Try pronouncing <u>unique New York</u> ten times fast.

The word <u>syzygy</u> refers to a straight line formed by three celestial bodies, as in the alignment of the earth, sun, and moon. [Quotation marks may also be used for words being defined.]

31

ABBREVIATIONS

The following guidelines on abbreviations pertain to the text of a nontechnical document. All academic disciplines use abbreviations in source citations, and much technical writing, such as in the sciences and engineering, uses many abbreviations in the document text. See Chapters 38–41 on source citations. Consult one of the style guides listed on pages 103–04 for the in-text requirements of the discipline you are writing in.

NOTE Usage varies, but writers increasingly omit periods from abbreviations of two or more words written in all-capital letters: *US, BA, USMC.* See page 52.

31a. Titles before and after proper names

BEFORE THE NAME	AFTER THE NAME
Dr. James Hsu	James Hsu, MD
Mr., Mrs., Ms., Hon.,	DDS, DVM, Ph.D.,
St., Rev., Msgr., Gen.	Ed.D., OSB, SJ, Sr., Jr.

Do not use abbreviations such as *Rev., Hon., Prof., Rep., Sen., Dr.,* and *St.* (for *Saint*) unless they appear before a proper name.

31b. Familiar abbreviations

Abbreviations using initials are acceptable in most writing as long as they are familiar to readers.

INSTITUTIONS	LSU, UCLA, TCU
ORGANIZATIONS	CIA, FBI, YMCA, AFL-CIO
CORPORATIONS	IBM, CBS, ITT
PEOPLE	JFK, LBJ, FDR
COUNTRIES	U.S.A. (or USA)

NOTE If a name or term (such as *operating room*) appears often in a piece of writing, then its abbreviation (*OR*) can cut down on extra words. Spell out the full term at its first appearance, indicate its abbreviation in parentheses, and then use the abbreviation.

31c. *BC, AD, AM, PM, no.,* and *$*

Use certain abbreviations only with specific dates or numbers.

31c

| 44 BC | 11:26 AM (*or* a.m.) | no. 36 (*or* No. 36) |
| AD 1492 | 8:05 PM (*or* p.m.) | $7.41 |

The abbreviation BC ("before Christ") always follows a date, whereas AD (*anno Domini*, Latin for "in the year of the Lord") precedes a date.

NOTE BCE ("before the common era") and CE ("common era") are increasingly replacing BC and AD, respectively. Both follow the date.

31d. Latin abbreviations

Generally, use the common Latin abbreviations (without underlining) only in source citations and comments in parentheses.

i.e.	*id est:*	that is
cf.	*confer:*	compare
e.g.	*exempli gratia:*	for example
et al.	*et alii:*	and others
etc.	*et cetera:*	and so forth
NB	*nota bene:*	note well

He said he would be gone a fortnight (i.e., two weeks).
Bloom et al., editors, *Anthology of Light Verse*

31e. Words usually spelled out

In most academic, general, and business writing, certain words should always be spelled out. (In technical writing, however, these words are more often abbreviated.)

NOTE Always spell out *and* (rather than using &) unless the symbol appears in a business name.

UNITS OF MEASUREMENT
The dog is thirty *inches* (not *in.*) high.
It once swam two *miles* (not *mi.*) across a lake.

GEOGRAPHICAL NAMES
The publisher is in *Massachusetts* (not *Mass.* or *MA*).
It moved from *Canada* (not *Can.*).

NAMES OF DAYS, MONTHS, AND HOLIDAYS
The truce was signed on *Tuesday* (not *Tues.*), *April* (not *Apr.*) 16.

It was ratified by *Christmas* (not *Xmas*).

NAMES OF PEOPLE
Robert (not *Robt.*) Frost writes accessible poems.
Virginia (not *Va.*) Woolf was British.

31e

The writer teaches *political science* (not *poli. sci.*).
She received an *economics* (not *econ.*) degree.

32
NUMBERS

This chapter addresses the use of numbers (numerals versus words) in the text of a document. All disciplines use many more numerals in source citations (see Chapters 38–41).

32a. Numerals vs. words

Always use numerals for numbers that require more than two words to spell out.

The leap year has *366* days.
The population of Minot, North Dakota, is about *32,800*.

In nontechnical academic writing, spell out numbers of one or two words.

The ball game drew *forty-two thousand* people. [A hyphenated number may be considered one word.]

In much business writing, use numerals for all numbers over ten (*five reasons, 11 participants*). In technical academic and business writing, such as in science and engineering, use numerals for all numbers over ten, and use numerals for zero through nine when they refer to exact measurements (*2 liters, 1 hour*). (Technical usage does vary from discipline to discipline. Consult one of the style guides listed on pp. 103–04 for more details.)

NOTE Use a combination of numerals and words for round numbers over a million: *26 million, 2.45 billion.* And use either all figures or all words when several numbers appear together in a passage, even if convention would require a mixture.

32b. Commonly used numerals

In nontechnical writing, numerals are conventional for certain information, even when the numbers could be spelled out in one or two words.

32b

DAYS AND YEARS

June 18, 1985   AD 12
1999   456 BC

PAGES, CHAPTERS, VOLUMES, ACTS, SCENES, LINES

Chapter 9, page 123
Hamlet, Act 5, Scene 3
Statistics, Volume 2

ADDRESSES

355 Clinton Avenue
Washington, DC 20036

EXACT AMOUNTS OF MONEY

$3.5 million $4.50

DECIMALS, PERCENTAGES, AND FRACTIONS

22.5   3½
48% (*or* 48 percent)

SCORES AND STATISTICS

a ratio of 8 to 1   21 to 7

THE TIME OF DAY

9:00   3:45

32c. Beginnings of sentences

For clarity, spell out any number that begins a sentence. If the number requires more than two words, reword the sentence so that the number falls later and can be expressed as a numeral.

32c

FAULTY   *103* visitors asked for refunds.

AWKWARD   *One hundred three* visitors asked for refunds.

REVISED   Of the visitors, *103* asked for refunds.

V

USING AND DOCUMENTING SOURCES

33. Evaluation and Synthesis of Sources *95*
34. Notes: Summary, Paraphrase, Direct Quotation *96*
35. Plagiarism *98*
36. Introduction of Borrowed Material *101*
37. Documentation of Sources *103*
38. MLA Documentation Style *104*
39. *Chicago Manual* Documentation Style *118*
40. APA Documentation Style *125*
41. CBE Documentation Style *134*

EVALUATION AND SYNTHESIS
OF SOURCES

The work of others can help you form, support, and extend your own ideas. Using sources requires, first, that you evaluate them and, second, that you discover relationships among them.

33a. Evaluation

To evaluate sources, scan introductions, tables of contents, and headings. Look for information about authors' backgrounds that will help you understand their expertise and bias. Try to answer the following questions about each source:

- Is the work relevant?

  Does the source devote some attention to your topic?
  Where in the source are you likely to find relevant information or ideas?
  Is the source appropriately specialized for your needs? Check the source's treatment of a topic you know something about, to ensure that it is neither too superficial nor too technical.
  How important is the source likely to be for your writing?

- Is the work reliable?

  How up to date is the source? If the publication date is not recent, be sure that other sources will give you more current views.
  Is the author an expert in the field? Look for an author biography, or look up the author in a biographical reference.
  What is the author's bias? Check biographical information or the author's own preface or introduction. Consider what others have written about the author or the source. (To find such commentary, ask your librarian for citation indexes or book review indexes.)
  Whatever his or her bias, does the author reason soundly, provide adequate evidence, and consider opposing views?

Don't expect to find harmony among sources, for reasonable people often disagree in their opinions. Thus you must deal honestly with the gaps and conflicts in sources. Old sources, superficial ones, slanted ones—these should be offset in your research and your writing by sources that are newer, more thorough, or more objective.

33b. Synthesis

SYNTHESIS is the process of forging relationships—in research writing, relationships among the ideas in sources. For instance, how do two writers' studies differ, or how do two poems by one writer compare? With synthesis, you create new knowledge.

A common trap of research writing is allowing your sources to control you, rather than vice versa. Avoid this trap by asking how each source contributes to the idea you are building. When taking notes, record connections between sources as well as data and other information. Also record your own reactions, such as your impression of a writer's theories. When drafting your paper, make sure each paragraph focuses on a conclusion you have drawn from your reading (the support for the idea will come from your sources). In this way, your paper will synthesize existing work into something wholly your own.

34
NOTES: SUMMARY, PARAPHRASE, DIRECT QUOTATION

Taking notes from sources is not a mechanical process of copying from books and periodicals. Rather, as you read and take notes you assess and organize the information in your sources. Researchers generally rely on the techniques discussed below.

NOTE See Chapter 36 for advice on integrating summaries, paraphrases, and direct quotations into your own sentences. See Chapters 37–41 for advice on documenting any material you borrow from another source.

34a. Summary

When you SUMMARIZE, you condense an extended idea or argument into a sentence or more in your own words. Summary is most useful when you want to record the gist of an author's idea without the background or supporting evidence. Here, for example, is a passage summarized in a sentence.

ORIGINAL

Generalizing about male and female styles of management is a tricky business, because stereotypes have traditionally been used to keep women down. Not too long ago it was a widely accepted truth that women were unstable, indecisive, temperamental and manipulative and weren't good team members because they'd never played football. In fighting off these prejudices many women simply tried to adopt masculine traits in the office.

—ANN HUGHEY and ERIC GELMAN, "Managing the Woman's Way," *Newsweek*, page 47

SUMMARY

Rather than be labeled with the sexist stereotypes that prevented their promotions, many women adopted masculine qualities.

34b. Paraphrase

When you PARAPHRASE, you follow much more closely the author's original presentation, but you still restate it in your own words. Paraphrase is most useful when you want to reconstruct an author's line of reasoning but don't feel the original words merit direct quotation. Here is a paraphrase of the passage above by Hughey and Gelman.

34c

PARAPHRASE

Because of the risk of stereotyping, which has served as a tool to block women from management, it is difficult to characterize a feminine management style. Women have been cited for their emotionality, instability, and lack of team spirit, among other qualities. Many women have defended themselves at work by adopting the qualities of men.

(Poor and revised paraphrases appear on pp. 99–100.)

34c. Direct quotation

If your purpose is to analyze a particular work, such as a short story or historical document, then you will use many direct quotations from the work. But otherwise you should quote from sources only in the following circumstances:

- The author's original satisfies one of these requirements:

  The language is unusually vivid, bold, or inventive.
  The quotation cannot be paraphrased without distortion or loss of meaning.
  The words themselves are at issue in your interpretation.
  The quotation represents and emphasizes the view of an important expert.
  The quotation is a graph, diagram, or table.

- The quotation is as short as possible.

  It includes only material relevant to your point.
  It is edited to eliminate examples and other unneeded material. (See below.)

When taking a quotation from a source, copy the material *carefully*. Take down the author's exact wording, spelling, capitalization, and punctuation. Proofread every direct quotation *at least twice*, and be sure you have supplied big quotation marks so that later you won't confuse the direct quotation with a paraphrase or summary. If you want to make changes for clarity, use brackets (see p. 69). If you want to omit irrelevant words or sentences, use ellipsis marks, usually three spaced periods (see pp. 67–68).

35

35

PLAGIARISM

PLAGIARISM (from a Latin word for "kidnapper") is the presentation of someone else's ideas or words as your own. Whether deliberate or accidental, plagiarism is a serious and often punishable offense.

- *Deliberate* plagiarism includes copying a sentence from a source and passing it off as your own, summarizing someone else's ideas without acknowledging your debt, or buying a term paper and handing it in as your own.
- *Accidental* plagiarism includes forgetting to place quotation marks around another writer's words, omitting a source citation because you are not aware of the need for it, or carelessly copying a source when you mean to paraphrase.

35a. What not to acknowledge

Your independent material

You are not required to acknowledge your own observations, thoughts, compilations of facts, or experimental
results, expressed in your own words and format.

Common knowledge

You need not acknowledge common knowledge: the
standard information of a field of study as well as folk literature and commonsense observations.

If you do not know a subject well enough to determine
whether a piece of information is common knowledge,
make a record of the source. As you read more about the
subject, the information may come up repeatedly without
acknowledgment, in which case it is probably common
knowledge. But if you are still in doubt when you finish
your research, always acknowledge the source.

35b. What to acknowledge

You must always acknowledge other people's independent material—that is, any facts or ideas that are not
common knowledge or your own. The source may be anything, including a book, an article, a movie, an interview,
a microfilmed document, or a computer program. You
must acknowledge not only ideas or facts themselves but
also the language and format in which the ideas or facts
appear, if you use them. That is, the wording, sentence
structures, arrangement of ideas, and special graphics
(such as a diagram) created by another writer belong to
that writer just as his or her ideas do.

35c

35c. How to avoid plagiarism

The following example baldly plagiarizes both the
structure and the words of the original quotation from
Jessica Mitford's *Kind and Usual Punishment*, page 9.

ORIGINAL	The character and mentality of the keepers may be of more importance in understanding prisons than the character and mentality of the kept.
PLAGIARISM	But the character of prison officials (the keepers) is more important in understanding prisons than the character of prisoners (the kept).

The next example is more subtle plagiarism, because it changes Mitford's sentence structure. But it still uses her words.

PLAGIARISM   In understanding prisons, we should know more about the character and mentality of the keepers than of the kept.

The plagiarism in these examples can be remedied by placing Mitford's exact words in quotation marks, changing her sentence structure when not quoting, and citing the source properly (here, in MLA style).

REVISION (QUOTATION)   According to one critic of the penal system, "The character and mentality of the keepers may be of more importance in understanding prisons than the character and mentality of the kept" (Mitford 9).

REVISION (PARAPHRASE)   One critic of the penal system maintains that we may be able to learn more about prisons from the psychology of the prison officials than from that of the prisoners (Mitford 9).

The following checklist can help you avoid plagiarism:

35c

* What type of source are you using: your own independent material, common knowledge, or someone else's independent material? You must acknowledge someone else's material.
* If you are quoting someone else's material, is the quotation exact? Have you inserted quotation marks around quotations run into the text? Have you shown omissions with ellipsis marks and additions with brackets?
* If you are paraphrasing or summarizing someone else's material, have you used your own words and sentence structures, not the source author's? Does your paraphrase or summary employ quotation marks when you resort to the author's exact language? Have you represented the author's meaning without distortion?
* Is each use of someone else's material acknowledged in your text? Are all your source citations complete and accurate?
* Does your list of works cited include all the sources you have drawn from in writing your paper?

36

INTRODUCTION OF
BORROWED MATERIAL

When using summaries, paraphrases, and quotations, integrate them smoothly into your own sentences. In the passage below, the writer initially did not mesh the structures of her own and her source's sentences.

AWKWARD   One editor disagrees with this view and "a good reporter does not fail to separate opinions from facts" (Lyman 52).

REVISED   One editor disagrees with this view, <u>maintaining that</u> "a good reporter does not fail to separate opinions from facts" (Lyman 52).

Even when not conflicting with your own sentence structure, borrowed material will be ineffective if you merely dump it in readers' laps without explaining how you intend it to be understood.

DUMPED   Many news editors and reporters maintain that it is impossible to keep personal opinions from influencing the selection and presentation of facts. "True, news reporters, like everyone else, form impressions of what they see and hear. However, a good reporter does not fail to separate opinions from facts" (Lyman 52).

REVISED   Many news editors and reporters maintain that it is impossible to keep personal opinions from influencing the selection and presentation of facts. <u>Yet not all authorities agree with this view. One editor grants that</u> "news reporters, like everyone else, form impressions of what they see and hear." <u>But, he insists</u>, "a good reporter does not fail to separate opinions from facts" (Lyman 52).

You can add other information to integrate a quotation and inform readers why you are using it:

AUTHOR NAMED   . . . <u>Harold Lyman</u> grants that "news reporters, like everyone else, form impressions of what they see and hear." But, Lyman insists, "a good reporter does not fail to separate opinions from facts" (52).

TITLE GIVEN ... Harold Lyman, in his book *The Conscience of the Journalist*, grants that "news reporters, like everyone else, form impressions of what they see and hear." But, Lyman insists, "a good reporter does not fail to separate opinions from facts" (52).

CREDENTIALS GIVEN ... Harold Lyman, a newspaper editor for more than forty years, grants that "news reporters, like everyone else, form impressions of what they see and hear." But, Lyman insists, "a good reporter does not fail to separate opinions from facts" (52).

The verbs *grants* and *insists* in the passages above tell the reader something about the source's attitudes in the quotations that follow: *grants* implies concession, and *insists* implies argument. Below is a list of verbs that can help you integrate and clarify borrowed material:

AUTHOR IS NEUTRAL	AUTHOR INFERS OR SUGGESTS	AUTHOR ARGUES	AUTHOR IS UNEASY OR DISPARAGING
comments	analyzes	claims	belittles
describes	asks	contends	bemoans
explains	assesses	defends	complains
illustrates	believes	disagrees	condemns
mentions	concludes	holds	deplores
notes	considers	insists	deprecates
observes	finds	maintains	derides
points out	predicts		laments
records	proposes	AUTHOR AGREES	warns
relates	reveals	accepts	
reports	shows	admits	
says	speculates	agrees	
sees	suggests	concedes	
thinks	supposes	concurs	
writes		grants	

You need not name the author, source, or credentials in your text when you are simply establishing facts or weaving together facts and opinions from varied sources (although, of course, you must still acknowledge each source in a citation).

NOTE See pages 62–63 and 65–66 for how to punctuate quotations. And see pages 63–64 for when to display long quotations separately from your text.

37
DOCUMENTATION OF SOURCES

Every time you borrow the words, facts, or ideas of others, you must DOCUMENT the source—that is, supply a reference (or document) telling readers that you borrowed the material and where you borrowed it from. (For guidelines on when sources must be documented, see Chapter 35.)

Editors and teachers in most academic disciplines require special documentation formats (or styles) in their scholarly journals and in students' papers. All the styles use a citation in the text that serves two purposes: it signals that material is borrowed, and it refers readers to detailed information about the source so that they can locate both the source and the place in the source where the borrowed material appears. The detailed source information appears either in footnotes or at the end of the paper.

Aside from these essential similarities, the disciplines' documentation styles differ markedly in citation form, arrangement of source information, and other particulars. Each discipline's style reflects the needs of its practitioners for certain kinds of information presented in certain ways—for instance, in-text citations in the social sciences indicate the date of the source's publication because currency is important.

This book details four documentation styles:

- MLA style, used in English, foreign languages, and some other humanities (Chapter 38)
- *Chicago Manual* style, used in history, art history, and some other disciplines (Chapter 39)
- APA style, used in psychology, educational psychology, and other social sciences (Chapter 40)
- CBE style, used in the biological and physical sciences and in mathematics (Chapter 41)

Beyond this book several guides outline other documentation styles:

American Anthropological Association. "Style Guide and Information for Authors." *American Anthropologist* (1977): 774–79.

American Chemical Society. *ACS Style Guide: A Manual for Authors and Editors.* 1986.

American Institute of Physics. *Style Manual for Guidance in the Preparation of Papers.* 4th ed. 1990.

American Mathematical Society. *A Manual for Authors of Mathematical Papers.* 8th ed. 1980.

American Medical Association. *Style Book: Editorial Manual.* 6th ed. 1976.

American Sociological Association. "Editorial Guidelines." Inside front cover of each issue of *American Sociological Review.*

Ask your instructor which style he or she prefers.

38
MLA DOCUMENTATION STYLE

Widely used in English, foreign languages, and other humanities, the MLA documentation style originates with the Modern Language Association. It appears in the *MLA Handbook for Writers of Research Papers,* 4th edition (1995), and the more recent *MLA Style Manual and Guide to Scholarly Publishing,* 2nd edition (1998). In MLA style brief parenthetical citations in the text (38a) direct readers to a list of works cited at the end of the text (38b).

38a. MLA parenthetical citations

38a

Citation formats

The in-text citations of sources must include just enough information for the reader to locate (1) the appropriate source in your list of works cited and (2) the place in the source where the borrowed material appears. Usually, you can meet both these requirements by providing the author's last name and the page(s) in the source on which the borrowed material appears.

1. AUTHOR NOT NAMED IN YOUR TEXT

One researcher concludes that "women impose a distinctive construction on moral problems, seeing moral dilemmas in terms of conflicting responsibilities" (Gilligan 105).

2. AUTHOR NAMED IN YOUR TEXT

One researcher, Carol Gilligan, concludes that "women impose a distinctive construction on moral

Index to MLA Parenthetical Citations

1. Author not named in your text *104*
2. Author named in your text *104*
3. A work with two or three authors *105*
4. A work with more than three authors *105*
5. An entire work (no page numbers) *105*
6. A multivolume work *105*
7. A work by an author of two or more cited works *106*
8. An unsigned work *106*
9. A government document or a work with a corporate author *106*
10. A source referred to by another source *106*
11. A literary work *106*
12. More than one work *106*
13. An electronic source *107*

problems, seeing moral dilemmas in terms of conflicting responsibilities" (105).

3. A WORK WITH TWO OR THREE AUTHORS

As Frieden and Sagalyn observe, "The poor and the minorities were the leading victims of highway and renewal programs" (29).

38a

4. A WORK WITH MORE THAN THREE AUTHORS

It took the combined forces of the Americans, Europeans, and Japanese to break the rebel siege of Beijing in 1900 (Lopez et al. 362).

5. AN ENTIRE WORK (NO PAGE NUMBERS)

Boyd deals with the need to acknowledge and come to terms with our fear of nuclear technology.

6. A MULTIVOLUME WORK

After issuing the Emancipation Proclamation, Lincoln said, "What I did, I did after very full deliberations, and under a very heavy and solemn sense of responsibility" (5: 438).

7. A WORK BY AN AUTHOR OF TWO OR MORE CITED WORKS

At about age seven, most children begin to use appropriate gestures to reinforce their stories
(Gardner, <u>Arts</u> 144-45).

8. AN UNSIGNED WORK

One article notes that a death-row inmate may de-
mand his own execution to achieve a fleeting notoriety ("Right").

9. A GOVERNMENT DOCUMENT OR A WORK WITH A CORPORATE AUTHOR

A 1995 report by the Hawaii Department of Education predicts a slow increase in enrollments (6).

10. A SOURCE REFERRED TO BY ANOTHER SOURCE

George Davino maintains that "even small children
have vivid ideas about nuclear energy" (qtd. in
Boyd 22).

11. A LITERARY WORK

Toward the end of James's novel, Maggie suddenly
feels "the intimate, the immediate, the familiar,
as she hadn't had them for so long" (535; pt. 6,
ch. 41).

Later in <u>King Lear</u> Shakespeare has the disguised
Edgar say, "The prince of darkness is a gentleman"
(3.4.147).

The citation above lists act number, scene number, and
line number, respectively.

12. MORE THAN ONE WORK

Two recent articles point out that a computer
badly used can be less efficient than no computer
at all (Gough and Hall 201; Richards 162).

13. An electronic source

```
Twins reared apart report similar feelings (Pal-
trey, pars. 6-7).
```

This source uses paragraph numbers, not page numbers. For a source using page numbers, follow model 1 or 2. For a source with no paragraph or page numbers, follow model 5. For a source with no author, follow model 8 or 9 (that is, name the title or site in place of an author).

Footnotes or endnotes in special circumstances

Footnotes or endnotes may supplement parenthetical citations when you cite several sources at once, when you comment on a source, or when you provide information that does not fit easily in the text. Signal a footnote or endnote in your text with a numeral raised above the appropriate line. Then write a note with the same numeral.

Text   At least five subsequent studies have confirmed these results.[1]

Note   [1] Abbott and Winger 266-68; Casner 27; Hoyenga 78-79; Marino 36; Tripp, Tripp, and Walk 179-83.

38b

If the note appears as a footnote, place it at the bottom of the page on which the citation appears, set it off from the text with quadruple spacing, and single-space the note itself. If the note appears as an endnote, place it in numerical order with the other endnotes on a page between the text and the list of works cited; double-space all the endnotes.

38b. MLA list of works cited

At the end of your paper, a list titled "Works Cited" includes all the sources you quoted, paraphrased, or summarized in your paper. The format of the list's first page is illustrated on page 110. Arrange your sources in alphabetical order by the last name of the author. If an author is not given in the source, alphabetize the source by the first main word of the title (excluding *A, An*, or *The*). In the models that follow for various sources, note these main features:

- Double-space all entries. Type the first line of each entry at the left margin, and indent all subsequent lines one-half inch or five spaces.
- List the author's name last-name first. If there are two or three authors, list all names after the first in normal order. Separate the names with commas.
- Give full titles, capitalizing all important words (see p. 87). (For periodical titles, omit any *A*, *An*, or *The*.) Underline the titles of books and periodicals; place titles of periodical articles in quotation marks.
- Provide publication information after the title. For books, give place of publication, publisher's name, and date. (Shorten publishers' names—for instance, *Little* for Little, Brown and *Harvard UP* for Harvard Univer-

---

Index to MLA Works-Cited Models

BOOKS
1. A book with one author *109*
2. A book with two or three authors *110*
3. A book with more than three authors *110*
4. Two or more works by the same author(s) *110*
5. A book with an editor *110*
6. A book with an author and an editor *111*
7. A translation *111*
8. A book with a corporate author *111*
9. An anonymous book *111*
10. A later edition *111*
11. A book with a title in its title *111*
12. A work in more than one volume *111*
13. A work in a series *112*
14. A selection from an anthology or collection *112*
15. Two or more selections from the same anthology *112*
16. An introduction, preface, foreword, or afterword *112*
17. An encyclopedia or almanac *112*

PERIODICALS
18. A signed article in a journal with continuous pagination throughout the annual volume *112*
19. A signed article in a journal that pages issues separately or that numbers only issues, not volumes *112*
20. A signed article in a monthly or bimonthly magazine *113*

sity Press.) For periodical articles, give the volume or issue number, date, and page numbers.
- Separate the main parts of an entry with periods followed by one space.

Books

1. A BOOK WITH ONE AUTHOR

Gilligan, Carol. <u>In a Different Voice: Psychological Theory and Women's Development</u>. Cambridge: Harvard UP, 1982.

21. A signed article in a weekly or biweekly magazine *113*
22. A signed article in a daily newspaper *113*
23. An unsigned article *113*
24. An editorial or letter to the editor *113*
25. A review *113*
26. An abstract of a dissertation *113*

ELECTRONIC SOURCES

27. A source on CD-ROM, diskette, or magnetic tape *114*
28. Electronic mail or an online posting *114*
29. An online scholarly project, reference database, or personal or professional site *115*
30. An online book *115*
31. An article in an online periodical *116*
32. A synchronous communication (MUD, MOO, etc.) *116*
33. Computer software *116*

OTHER SOURCES

34. A government document *116*
35. A musical composition or work of art *117*
36. A film or video recording *117*
37. A television or radio program *117*
38. A performance *117*
39. A recording *117*
40. A letter *117*
41. A lecture or address *118*
42. An interview *118*

38b

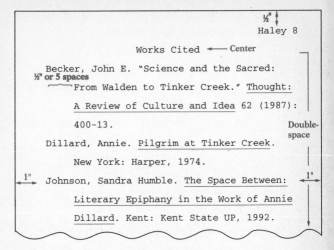

½" ↕
Haley 8

Works Cited ◄—— Center

Becker, John E. "Science and the Sacred:
½" or 5 spaces
From Walden to Tinker Creek." Thought:

A Review of Culture and Idea 62 (1987):

400-13.   Double-
space

Dillard, Annie. Pilgrim at Tinker Creek.

New York: Harper, 1974.

←1"→ Johnson, Sandra Humble. The Space Between: ←1"→

Literary Epiphany in the Work of Annie

Dillard. Kent: Kent State UP, 1992.

2. A BOOK WITH TWO OR THREE AUTHORS

Frieden, Bernard J., and Lynne B. Sagalyn. Down-

town, Inc.: How America Rebuilds Cities. Cam-

bridge: MIT, 1989.

3. A BOOK WITH MORE THAN THREE AUTHORS

Lopez, Robert S., et al. Civilizations: Western

and World. Boston: Little, 1975.

4. TWO OR MORE WORKS BY THE SAME AUTHOR(S)

Gardner, Howard. The Arts and Human Development.

New York: Wiley, 1973.

---. The Quest for Mind: Piaget, Lévi-Strauss, and

the Structuralist Movement. New York: Knopf,

1973.

5. A BOOK WITH AN EDITOR

Ruitenbeek, Hendrick, ed. Freud as We Knew Him.

Detroit: Wayne State UP, 1973.

38b

6. A BOOK WITH AN AUTHOR AND AN EDITOR

Melville, Herman. The Confidence Man: His Masquer-
     ade. Ed. Hershel Parker. New York: Norton,
     1971.

7. A TRANSLATION

Alighieri, Dante. The Inferno. Trans. John Ciardi.
     New York: NAL, 1971.

8. A BOOK WITH A CORPORATE AUTHOR

Lorenz, Inc. Research in Social Studies Teaching.
     Baltimore: Arrow, 1992.

9. AN ANONYMOUS BOOK

Merriam-Webster's Collegiate Dictionary. 10th ed.
     Springfield: Merriam-Webster, 1993.

10. A LATER EDITION

Bollinger, Dwight L. Aspects of Language. 2nd ed.
     New York: Harcourt, 1975.

11. A BOOK WITH A TITLE IN ITS TITLE

Eco, Umberto. Postscript to The Name of the Rose.
     Trans. William Weaver. New York: Harcourt,
     1983.

12. A WORK IN MORE THAN ONE VOLUME

Lincoln, Abraham. The Collected Works of Abraham
     Lincoln. Ed. Roy P. Basler. 8 vols. New
     Brunswick: Rutgers UP, 1953.

Lincoln, Abraham. The Collected Works of Abraham
     Lincoln. Ed. Roy P. Basler. Vol. 5. New
     Brunswick: Rutgers UP, 1953. 8 vols.

38b

13. A WORK IN A SERIES

Bergman, Ingmar. <u>The Seventh Seal</u>. Modern Film

    Scripts Series. New York: Simon, 1968.

14. A SELECTION FROM AN ANTHOLOGY OR COLLECTION

Plath, Sylvia. "Lorelei." <u>The Collected Poems</u>. By

    Sylvia Plath. Ed. Ted Hughes. New York: Har-

    per, 1981. 94-95.

15. TWO OR MORE SELECTIONS FROM THE SAME ANTHOLOGY

Brooks, Rosetta. "Streetwise." Martin 38-39.

Martin, Richard, ed. <u>The New Urban Landscape</u>. New

    York: Rizzoli, 1990.

Plotkin, Mark J. "Tropical Forests and the Urban

    Landscape." Martin 50-51.

16. AN INTRODUCTION, PREFACE, FOREWORD, OR AFTERWORD

Donaldson, Norman. Introduction. <u>The Claverings</u>.

    By Anthony Trollope. New York: Dover, 1977.

    vii-xv.

17. AN ENCYCLOPEDIA OR ALMANAC

"Mammoth." <u>The Columbia Encyclopedia</u>. 1993.

Mark, Herman F. "Polymers." <u>The New Encyclopaedia</u>

    <u>Britannica: Macropaedia</u>. 16th ed. 1991.

Periodicals: Journals, magazines, newspapers

18. A SIGNED ARTICLE IN A JOURNAL WITH CONTINUOUS PAGINATION THROUGHOUT THE ANNUAL VOLUME

Lever, Janet. "Sex Differences in the Games Children

    Play." <u>Social Problems</u> 23 (1976): 478-87.

19. A SIGNED ARTICLE IN A JOURNAL THAT PAGES ISSUES SEPARATE-LY OR THAT NUMBERS ONLY ISSUES, NOT VOLUMES

Dacey, June. "Management Participation in Corpo-

rate Buy-Outs." <u>Management Perspectives</u> 7.4
(1994): 20-31.

20. A SIGNED ARTICLE IN A MONTHLY OR BIMONTHLY MAGAZINE

Stein, Harry. "Living with Lies." <u>Esquire</u> Dec.
1981: 23.

21. A SIGNED ARTICLE IN A WEEKLY OR BIWEEKLY MAGAZINE

Stevens, Mark. "Low and Behold." <u>New Republic</u>
24 Dec. 1990: 27-33.

22. A SIGNED ARTICLE IN A DAILY NEWSPAPER

Ramirez, Anthony. "Computer Groups Plan Standards." <u>New York Times</u> 14 Dec. 1993, late
ed.: D5.

23. AN UNSIGNED ARTICLE

"The Right to Die." <u>Time</u> 11 Oct. 1976: 101.

24. AN EDITORIAL OR LETTER TO THE EDITOR

"Bodily Intrusions." Editorial. <u>New York Times</u>
29 Aug. 1990, late ed.: A20.

Dowding, Michael. Letter. <u>Economist</u> 5-11 Jan.
1985: 4.

25. A REVIEW

Dunne, John Gregory. "The Secret of Danny Santiago." Rev. of <u>Famous All over Town</u>, by Danny
Santiago. <u>New York Review of Books</u> 16 Aug.
1984: 17-27.

26. AN ABSTRACT OF A DISSERTATION

Steciw, Steven K. "Alterations to the Pessac Project of Le Corbusier." Diss. U of Cambridge,
England, 1986. <u>DAI</u> 46 (1986): 565C.

38b

114 · MLA documentation style

Electronic sources

Electronic sources include those available on CD-ROM, diskette, or magnetic tape and those available online, as through the Internet. The models below follow the most recent and extensive MLA guidelines, from the *MLA Style Manual and Guide to Scholarly Publishing*.

NOTE Online sources require two special pieces of information:

• Give the date when you consulted the source as well as the date when the source was posted online. The posting date comes first, with other publication information. Your access date falls near the end of the entry, just before the electronic address.

• Give the source's exact and complete electronic address, enclosed in angle brackets (< >). Place the address at the end of the entry. If you must break an address from one line to the next, do so *only* after a slash, and do not hyphenate.

27. A SOURCE ON CD-ROM, DISKETTE, OR MAGNETIC TAPE

CD-ROM periodical also published in print:

```
Ramirez, Anthony. "Computer Groups Plan Stan-
     dards." New York Times 14 Dec. 1993, late
     ed.: D5. New York Times Ondisc. CD-ROM.
     UMI-Proquest. June 1994.
```

CD-ROM periodical not published in print:

```
"Vanguard Forecasts." Business Outlook. CD-ROM.
     Information Access. May 1994.
```

Nonperiodical CD-ROM, diskette, or tape:

```
Shelley, Mary Wollstonecraft. Frankenstein. Clas-
     sic Library. CD-ROM. Alameda: Andromeda,
     1993.
```

28. ELECTRONIC MAIL OR AN ONLINE POSTING

Electronic mail:

```
Millon, Michele. "Re: Grief Therapy." E-mail to
     the author. 4 May 1997.
```

An e-mail discussion list:

Tourville, Michael. "European Currency Reform."

6 Jan. 1997. Online posting. International

Finance Discussion List. 23 Feb. 1997

<http://www.weg.isu.edu/finance-dl/>.

A newsgroup:

Cramer, Sherry. "Recent Investment Practices."

26 Mar. 1997. Online posting. 3 Apr. 1997

<news:biz.investment.current.2700>.

29. AN ONLINE SCHOLARLY PROJECT, REFERENCE DATABASE, OR PERSONAL OR PROFESSIONAL SITE

A scholarly project or database:

Scots Teaching and Research Network. Ed. John Cor-

bett. 2 Feb. 1998. U of Glasgow. 5 Mar. 1998

<http://www.arts.gla.ac.uk/www/english/comet/

starn.htm>.

A short work within a scholarly project:

Barbour, John. "The Brus." Scots Teaching and Re-

search Network. Ed. John Corbett. 2 Feb.

1998. U of Glasgow. 5 Mar. 1998 <http://

www/arts.gla.ac.uk/www/english/comet/starn/

poetry/brus/contents.htm>.

A personal or professional site:

Lederman, Leon. Topics in Modern Physics--Leder-

man. 12 Dec. 1997 <http://www-ed.fnal.gov/

samplers/hsphys/people/lederman.html>.

30. AN ONLINE BOOK

James, Henry. The Turn of the Screw. New York:

Scribner's, 1908-09. 4 Mar. 1998 <http://

www.americanliterature.com/TS/TSINDX.HTML>.

38b

31. AN ARTICLE IN AN ONLINE PERIODICAL

An article in a scholarly journal:

Palfrey, Andrew. "Choice of Mates in Identical
	Twins." <u>Modern Psychology</u> 4.1 (1996): 12
	pars. 25 Feb. 1996 <http://www.liasu.edu/
	modpsy/palfrey4(1).htm>.

An article in a newspaper:

Still, Lucia. "On the Battlefields of Business,
	Millions of Casualties." <u>New York Times on the
	Web</u> 3 Mar. 1996. 17 Aug. 1996 <http://www
	.nytimes.com/specials/downsize/
	03down1.html>.

An article in a magazine:

Palevitz, Barry A., and Ricki Lewis. "Death Raises
	Safety Issues for Primate Handlers." <u>Scien-
	tist</u> 2 Mar. 1998: 1+. 27 Mar. 1998 <http://
	www.the-scientist.library.upenn.edu/yr1998/
	mar/palevitz_pl_980302.html>.

32. A SYNCHRONOUS COMMUNICATION (**MUD, MOO,** ETC.)

Bruckman, Amy. MediaMOO Symposium: Virtual Worlds
	for Business? 20 Jan. 1998. MediaMOO. 26 Feb.
	1998 <http://www.cc.gatech.edu/Amy.Bruckman/
	MediaMOO/cscw-symposium-98.html>.

33. COMPUTER SOFTWARE

<u>Project Scheduler 8000</u>. Ver. 3.1. Orlando: Scitor,
	1997.

Other sources

34. A GOVERNMENT DOCUMENT

United States. Cong. House. Committee on Ways and
	Means. <u>Medicare Payment for Outpatient Physi-</u>

cal and Occupational Therapy Services. 102nd

Cong., 1st sess. Washington: GPO, 1991.

35. A MUSICAL COMPOSITION OR WORK OF ART

Mozart, Wolfgang Amadeus. Piano Concerto no. 20 in

D Minor, K. 466.

Sargent, John Singer. Venetian Doorway. Metropoli-

tan Museum of Art, New York.

36. A FILM OR VIDEO RECORDING

Spielberg, Steven, dir. Schindler's List. Perf.

Liam Neeson and Ben Kingsley. Universal, 1993.

Serenade. Chor. George Balanchine. Perf. San Fran-

cisco Ballet. Dir. Hilary Beane. 1981. Video-

cassette. PBS Video, 1987.

37. A TELEVISION OR RADIO PROGRAM

A Life Together. With Donald Hall and Jane Kenyon.

Bill Moyers' Journal. PBS. WNET, New York.

17 Dec. 1993.

38c

38. A PERFORMANCE

The English Only Restaurant. By Silvio Martinez

Palau. Dir. Susana Tubert. Puerto Rican Trav-

eling Theater, New York. 27 July 1990.

Ozawa, Seiji, cond. Boston Symphony Orch. Concert.

Symphony Hall, Boston. 25 Apr. 1991.

39. A RECORDING

Mitchell, Joni. For the Roses. Asylum, 1972.

Brahms, Johannes. Concerto no. 2 in B-flat, op.

83. Perf. Artur Rubinstein. Cond. Eugene Or-

mandy. Philadelphia Orch. RCA, 1972.

40. A LETTER

Buttolph, Mrs. Laura E. Letter to Rev. and Mrs.

C. C. Jones. 20 June 1857. In <u>The Children of</u>
<u>Pride: A True Story of Georgia and the Civil</u>
<u>War</u>. Ed. Robert Manson Myers. New Haven: Yale
UP, 1972. 334.

Packer, Ann E. Letter to the author. 15 June 1988.

41. A LECTURE OR ADDRESS

Carlone, Dennis J. "Urban Design in the 1990s."
Sixth Symposium on Urban Issues. City of Cambridge. Cambridge City Hall, 16 Oct. 1988.

42. AN INTERVIEW

Graaf, Vera. Personal interview. 19 Dec. 1996.

Martin, William. Interview. "Give Me That Big Time
Religion." <u>Frontline</u>. PBS. WGBH, Boston. 13
Feb. 1984.

39
CHICAGO MANUAL DOCUMENTATION STYLE

39a

In history, art history, and many other disciplines, writers rely on *The Chicago Manual of Style*, 14th edition (1993), or the student reference adapted from it, *A Manual for Writers of Term Papers, Theses, and Dissertations,* by Kate L. Turabian, 6th edition revised by John Grossman and Alice Bennett (1996). Both books detail two documentation styles. One, used mainly by scientists and social scientists, closely resembles the style of the American Psychological Association, covered in the next chapter. The other style, used more in the humanities, calls for footnotes or endnotes and a bibliography. This style is described below.

39a. *Chicago Manual* endnotes or footnotes and works-cited entries

In the *Chicago Manual* note style, a raised numeral in the text refers the reader to source information in endnotes or footnotes. (Ask your instructor what kind of note you should use. Footnotes may be preferred because they

them.) At the end of the paper, a list titled "Works Cited" includes all sources in alphabetical order.

Whether providing footnotes or endnotes, use single spacing for each note and double spacing between notes. With footnotes, separate the notes from the text with a short line, as shown in the following sample:

In 1901, Madras, Bengal, and Punjab were a few of the huge Indian provinces governed by the British viceroy.⁶ British rule, observes Stuart Cary Welch, "seemed as permanent as Mount Everest."⁷

---

5 spaces

     6. Martin Gilbert, <u>Atlas of British History</u> (New York: Dorset Press, 1968), 96.] Single-space

← Double-space

     7. Stuart Cary Welch, <u>India: Art and Culture</u> (New York: Metropolitan Museum of Art, 1985), 421.] Single-space

↕ 1"

For the list of sources at the end of the paper, use the format on the next page. Arrange the sources alphabetically by the authors' last names.

Notes and works-cited entries differ in key ways:

NOTE

     6. Martin Gilbert, <u>Atlas of British History</u> (New York: Dorset Press, 1968), 96.

WORKS CITED

Gilbert, Martin. <u>Atlas of British History</u>. New York: Dorset Press, 1968.

- In the note, start with a number (typed on the line and followed by a period) that corresponds to the note number in the text. In the works-cited entry, omit any starting number.
- In the note, indent the first line five spaces. In the works-cited entry, indent the second and subsequent lines five spaces.

39a

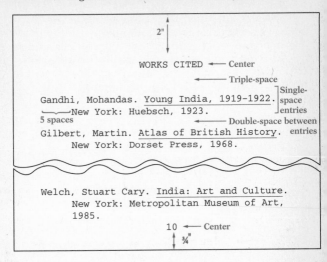

- In the note, give the author's name in normal order. In the works-cited entry, begin with the author's last name.
- In the note, use commas between elements such as author's name and title. In the works-cited entry, use periods between elements, followed by one space.
- In the note, enclose publication information in parentheses, with no preceding punctuation. In the works-cited entry, precede the publication information with a period and don't use parentheses.
- In the note, include the specific page number(s) you borrow from, omitting *p.* or *pp.* In the works-cited entry, which cites the entire source, omit page numbers except for entire parts of books or articles in periodicals.

Notes and works-cited entries also share certain features:

- Underline or italicize the titles of books and periodicals (ask your instructor for his or her preference).
- Enclose in quotation marks the titles of parts of books or articles in periodicals.
- Do not abbreviate publishers' names, but omit *Inc.*, *Co.*, and similar abbreviations.
- Do not use *p.* or *pp.* before page numbers.

39b. *Chicago Manual* models

In the following models for common sources, notes and works-cited entries appear together for easy refer-

39b

Index to *Chicago Manual* Note and Works-Cited Models

BOOKS
1. A book with one, two, or three authors *121*
2. A book with more than three authors *122*
3. A book with an editor *122*
4. An anonymous work *122*
5. A later edition *122*
6. A work in more than one volume *122*
7. A selection from an anthology *123*

PERIODICALS
8. An article in a journal with continuous pagination throughout the annual volume *123*
9. An article in a journal that pages issues separately *123*
10. An article in a popular magazine *123*
11. An article in a newspaper *123*

OTHER SOURCES
12. A government document *124*
13. A work of art *124*
14. A source on CD-ROM or diskette *124*
15. An online source *124*
16. Two or more citations of the same source *125*

39b

ence. Be sure to use the numbered note form for notes and the unnumbered works-cited form for works-cited entries.

Books

1. A BOOK WITH ONE, TWO, OR THREE AUTHORS

1. Carol Gilligan, In a Different Voice: Psychological Theory and Women's Development (Cambridge: Harvard University Press, 1982), 27.

Gilligan, Carol. In a Different Voice: Psychological Theory and Women's Development. Cambridge: Harvard University Press, 1982.

1. Bernard J. Frieden and Lynne B. Sagalyn, Downtown, Inc: How America Rebuilds Cities (Cambridge: MIT Press, 1989), 16.

Frieden, Bernard J., and Lynne B. Sagalyn. Downtown, Inc.: How America Rebuilds Cities. Cambridge: MIT Press, 1989.

2. A BOOK WITH MORE THAN THREE AUTHORS

    2. Joan Stryker and others, eds., Encyclope-
dia of American Life, 2d ed. (Boston: Winship,
1995), 126-28.

Stryker, Joan, William Hones, William Parker, and
 Sylvia Mannes, eds. Encyclopedia of American
 Life. 2d ed. Boston: Winship, 1995.

3. A BOOK WITH AN EDITOR

    3. Hendrick Ruitenbeek, ed., Freud as We Knew
Him (Detroit: Wayne State University Press, 1973),
64.

Ruitenbeek, Hendrick, ed. Freud as We Knew Him.
 Detroit: Wayne State University Press, 1973.

4. AN ANONYMOUS WORK

    4. Merriam-Webster's Collegiate Dictionary,
10th ed. (Springfield, Mass.: Merriam-Webster,
1993).

Merriam-Webster's Collegiate Dictionary. 10th ed.
 Springfield, Mass.: Merriam-Webster, 1993.

5. A LATER EDITION

    5. Dwight L. Bollinger, Aspects of Language,
2d ed. (New York: Harcourt Brace Jovanovich,
1975), 20.

Bollinger, Dwight L. Aspects of Language. 2d ed.
 New York: Harcourt Brace Jovanovich, 1975.

6. A WORK IN MORE THAN ONE VOLUME

    6. Abraham Lincoln, The Collected Works of
Abraham Lincoln, ed. Roy P. Basler (New Brunswick:
Rutgers University Press, 1953), 5:426-28.

Lincoln, Abraham. The Collected Works of Abraham
 Lincoln. Ed. Roy P. Basler. Vol. 5. New
 Brunswick: Rutgers University Press, 1953.

39b

7. A SELECTION FROM AN ANTHOLOGY

7. Rosetta Brooks, "Streetwise," in <u>The New Urban Landscape</u>, ed. Richard Martin (New York: Rizzoli, 1990), 38–39.

Brooks, Rosetta. "Streetwise." In <u>The New Urban Landscape</u>, ed. Richard Martin, 37-60. New York: Rizzoli, 1990.

Periodicals: Journals, magazines, newspapers

8. AN ARTICLE IN A JOURNAL WITH CONTINUOUS PAGINATION THROUGHOUT THE ANNUAL VOLUME

8. Janet Lever, "Sex Differences in the Games Children Play," <u>Social Problems</u> 23 (1976): 482.

Lever, Janet. "Sex Differences in the Games Children Play." <u>Social Problems</u> 23 (1976): 478-87.

9. AN ARTICLE IN A JOURNAL THAT PAGES ISSUES SEPARATELY

9. June Dacey, "Management Participation in Corporate Buy-Outs," <u>Management Perspectives</u> 7, no. 4 (1994): 22.

Dacey, June. "Management Participation in Corporate Buy-Outs." <u>Management Perspectives</u> 7, no. 4 (1994): 20-31.

10. AN ARTICLE IN A POPULAR MAGAZINE

10. Mark Stevens, "Low and Behold," <u>New Republic</u>, 24 December 1990, 28.

Stevens, Mark. "Low and Behold." <u>New Republic</u>, 24 December 1990, 27-33.

11. AN ARTICLE IN A NEWSPAPER

11. Anthony Ramirez, "Computer Groups Plan Standards," <u>New York Times</u>, 14 December 1993, D5, late edition.

Ramirez, Anthony. "Computer Groups Plan Standards." <u>New York Times</u>, 14 December 1993, D5, late edition.

Other sources

12. A GOVERNMENT DOCUMENT

12. House, <u>Medicare Payment for Outpatient Physical and Occupational Therapy Services</u>, 102d Cong., 1st sess., 1991, H. Doc. 409, 12-13.

U.S. House. <u>Medicare Payment for Outpatient Physical and Occupational Therapy Services</u>, 102d Cong., 1st sess., 1991. H. Doc. 409.

13. A WORK OF ART

13. John Singer Sargent, <u>In Switzerland</u>, watercolor, 1908, Metropolitan Museum of Art, New York.

Sargent, John Singer. <u>In Switzerland</u>, watercolor, 1908. Metropolitan Museum of Art, New York.

14. A SOURCE ON CD-ROM OR DISKETTE

14. Anthony Ramirez, "Computer Groups Plan Standards," <u>New York Times</u>, 14 December 1993, D5, <u>New York Times Ondisc</u> [CD-ROM], UMI-Proquest, June 1994.

Ramirez, Anthony. "Computer Groups Plan Standards." <u>New York Times</u>, 14 December 1993, D5. <u>New York Times Ondisc</u> [CD-ROM], UMI-Proquest, June 1994.

15. AN ONLINE SOURCE

15. Jane Austen, <u>Emma</u> [book online], ed. Ronald Blythe (Harmondsworth: Penguin, 1972), Oxford Text Archive, accessed 15 December 1995; available from ftp://ota.ox.ac.uk/public/english/Austen/emma.1519.

Austen, Jane. <u>Emma</u> [book online]. Ed. Ronald Blythe. Harmondsworth: Penguin, 1972. Oxford Text Archive. Accessed 15 December 1995. Available from ftp://ota.ox.ac.uk/public/english/Austen/emma.1519.

15. Andrew Palfrey, "Choice of Mates in Identical Twins," <u>Modern Psychology</u> 4, no. 1 (1996): pars. 7-8 [journal online], accessed 25 February 1996, available from http://www.liasu.edu/modpsy/palfrey4(1).htm.

Palfrey, Andrew. "Choice of Mates in Identical Twins." <u>Modern Psychology</u> 4, no. 1 (1996)

```
[journal online]. Accessed 25 February 1996.
Available from http://www.liasu.edu/modpsy/
palfrey4(1).htm.
```

16. TWO OR MORE CITATIONS OF THE SAME SOURCE

Reference to the same source cited in the preceding note:

```
     8. Janet Lever, "Sex Differences in the Games
Children Play," Social Problems 23 (1976): 482.
```

```
     9. Ibid., 483.
```

Reference to a source cited earlier than the preceding note:

```
     1. Carol Gilligan, In a Different Voice: Psy-
chological Theory and Women's Development (Cam-
bridge: Harvard University Press, 1982), 27.
```

```
     2. Carol Gilligan, "Moral Development in the
College Years," The Modern American College, ed.
A. Chickering (San Francisco: Jossey-Bass, 1981),
286.
```

```
     3. Gilligan, In a Different Voice, 47.
```

Omit the shortened title if you are using only one source by the cited author(s).

40
APA DOCUMENTATION STYLE

The documentation style of the American Psychological Association is used in psychology and some other social sciences and is very similar to the styles in sociology, economics, and other disciplines. The following adapts the APA style from the *Publication Manual of the American Psychological Association,* 4th edition (1994).

40a. APA parenthetical citations

Citation formats

In the APA style, parenthetical citations in the text refer to a list of sources at the end of the text. The basic parenthetical citation contains the author's last name, the date of publication, and often the page number from which material is borrowed.

Index to APA Parenthetical Citations

1. Author not named in your text *126*
2. Author named in your text *126*
3. A work with two authors *126*
4. A work with three to five authors *126*
5. A work with six or more authors *127*
6. A work with a corporate author *127*
7. An anonymous work *127*
8. One of two or more works by the same author(s) *127*
9. Two or more works by different authors *127*
10. A source referred to by another source *127*

1. AUTHOR NOT NAMED IN YOUR TEXT

One critic of Milgram's experiments insisted that the subjects "should have been fully informed of the possible effects on them" (Baumrind, 1968, p. 34).

2. AUTHOR NAMED IN YOUR TEXT

Baumrind (1968, p. 34) insisted that the subjects in Milgram's study "should have been fully informed of the possible effects on them."

3. A WORK WITH TWO AUTHORS

Pepinsky and DeStefano (1977) demonstrate that a teacher's language often reveals hidden biases.

One study (Pepinsky & DeStefano, 1977) demonstrates hidden biases in a teacher's language.

4. A WORK WITH THREE TO FIVE AUTHORS

First reference:

Pepinsky, Dunn, Rentl, and Corson (1973) further demonstrate the biases evident in gestures.

Later references:

In the work of Pepinsky et al. (1973), the loaded gestures include head shakes and eye contact.

5. A WORK WITH SIX OR MORE AUTHORS

One study (Rutter et al., 1976) attempts to explain these geographical differences in adolescent experience.

6. A WORK WITH A CORPORATE AUTHOR

An earlier prediction was even more somber (Lorenz, Inc., 1970).

7. AN ANONYMOUS WORK

One article ("Right to Die," 1976) noted that a death-row inmate may crave notoriety.

8. ONE OF TWO OR MORE WORKS BY THE SAME AUTHOR(S)

At about age seven, most children begin to use appropriate gestures to reinforce their stories (Gardner, 1973a, pp. 144-145).

(See the reference for this source on p. 131.)

40a

9. TWO OR MORE WORKS BY DIFFERENT AUTHORS

Two studies (Herskowitz, 1974; Marconi & Hamblen, 1980) found that periodic safety instruction can dramatically reduce employees' accidents.

10. A SOURCE REFERRED TO BY ANOTHER SOURCE

Supporting data appear in a study by Wong (cited in Marconi & Hamblen, 1980).

Footnotes for supplementary content

When you need to explain something in your text—for instance, commenting on a source or providing data that don't fit into the relevant paragraph—you may place the supplementary information in a footnote. Follow the instructions for footnotes in the *Chicago Manual* style (pp. 118–20). Be careful not to overuse such notes: they can be more distracting than helpful.

40b. APA reference list

In APA style, the in-text parenthetical citations refer to the list of sources at the end of the text. In this list, titled "References," you include full publication information on every source cited in your paper. The reference list falls at the end of the paper, numbered in sequence with the preceding pages. The sample below shows the elements and their spacing.

```
     Shortened title and
     page number (see p. 80) ──────► Dating Violence        8

                    References ◄── Center

    Cates, R. L., Rutter, C. H., Karl, J., Linton,

    ┌──────┘ M., & Smith, K. (1982). Premarital abuse:
    5 spaces
             A social psychological perspective.          Double-
                                                           space
             Journal of Family Issues, 3(1), 79-90.

    Glaser, R., and Rutter, C. H. (Eds.). (1984).

             Familial violence [Special issue].

             Family Relations, 33.
```

Prepare APA references as follows:

• Arrange the sources alphabetically by the author's last name or, if there is no author, by the first main word of the title.
• Double-space all entries.
• Type the first line of each entry at the left margin, and indent all subsequent lines five spaces. (This so-called hanging indent is clearest for student papers. For manuscripts that will be published, the APA specifies an indention for the first line and not the others.)
• List all authors last-name first, separating names and parts of names with commas. Use initials for first and middle names. Use an ampersand (&) rather than *and* before the last author's name.

Index to APA References

BOOKS

1. A book with one author *130*
2. A book with two or more authors *130*
3. A book with an editor *130*
4. A book with a translator *130*
5. A book with a corporate author *130*
6. An anonymous book *130*
7. Two or more works by the same author(s) published in the same year *131*
8. A later edition *131*
9. A work in more than one volume *131*
10. An article or chapter in an edited book *131*

PERIODICALS

11. An article in a journal with continuous pagination throughout the annual volume *131*
12. An article in a journal that pages issues separately *132*
13. An article in a magazine *132*
14. An article in a newspaper *132*
15. An unsigned article *132*
16. A review *132*

OTHER SOURCES

17. A report *132*
18. An information service *132*
19. A government document *133*
20. An interview *133*
21. A videotape, recording, performance, or other audiovisual source *133*
22. Computer software or a source on CD-ROM *133*
23. An online source *133*

40b

- Place the date of publication in parentheses after the author's name.
- In titles of books and articles, capitalize only the first word of the title, the first word of the subtitle, and proper names; all other words begin with small letters. In titles of journals, capitalize all significant words.
- Underline the titles of books and periodicals, along with any comma or period following. Also underline volume numbers of journals. Do not underline or use quotation marks around the titles of periodical articles.

- Give full names of university presses and of associations acting as publishers. Give brief names for other publishers, omitting first names (*Wiley* instead of *John Wiley*) and *Co.*, *Inc.*, and the like.
- Use the abbreviation *p.* or *pp.* before page numbers in books and newspapers, but *not* in other periodicals. For inclusive page numbers, include all figures: *667–668*.
- Separate the parts of the reference (author, date, title, and publication information) with a period and one space.

Books

1. A BOOK WITH ONE AUTHOR

Rodriguez, R. (1982). <u>A hunger of memory: The education of Richard Rodriguez.</u> Boston: Godine.

2. A BOOK WITH TWO OR MORE AUTHORS

Nesselroade, J. R., & Baltes, P. B. (1979). <u>Longitudinal research in the study of behavioral development.</u> New York: Academic.

3. A BOOK WITH AN EDITOR

Dohrenwend, B. S., & Dohrenwend, B. P. (Eds.). (1974). <u>Stressful life events: Their nature and effects.</u> New York: Wiley.

4. A BOOK WITH A TRANSLATOR

Trajan, P. D. (1927). <u>Psychology of animals.</u> (H. Simone, Trans.). Washington, DC: Halperin.

5. A BOOK WITH A CORPORATE AUTHOR

Lorenz, Inc. (1992). <u>Research in social studies teaching.</u> Baltimore: Arrow.

6. AN ANONYMOUS BOOK

<u>Merriam-Webster's collegiate dictionary</u> (10th ed.). (1993). Springfield, MA: Merriam-Webster.

7. TWO OR MORE WORKS BY THE SAME AUTHOR(S) PUBLISHED IN THE SAME YEAR

Gardner, H. (1973a). The arts and human development. New York: Wiley.

Gardner, H. (1973b). The quest for mind: Piaget,
Lévi-Strauss, and the structuralist movement.
New York: Knopf.

8. A LATER EDITION

Bollinger, D. L. (1975). Aspects of language (2nd
ed.). New York: Harcourt Brace Jovanovich.

9. A WORK IN MORE THAN ONE VOLUME

Lincoln, A. (1953). The collected works of Abraham
Lincoln (R. P. Basler, Ed.). (Vol. 5). New
Brunswick, NJ: Rutgers University Press.

Lincoln, A. (1953). The collected works of Abraham
Lincoln (R. P. Basler, Ed.). (Vols. 1-8). New
Brunswick, NJ: Rutgers University Press.

10. AN ARTICLE OR CHAPTER IN AN EDITED BOOK

Paykel, E. S. (1974). Life stress and psychiatric
disorder: Applications of the clinical ap-
proach. In B. S. Dohrenwend & B. P. Dohrenwend (Eds.), Stressful life events: Their
nature and effects (pp. 239-264). New York:
Wiley.

Periodicals: Journals, magazines, newspapers

11. AN ARTICLE IN A JOURNAL WITH CONTINUOUS PAGINATION THROUGHOUT THE ANNUAL VOLUME

Emery, R. E. (1982). Marital turmoil: Interper-
sonal conflict and the children of divorce.
Psychological Bulletin, 92, 310-330.

40b

12. AN ARTICLE IN A JOURNAL THAT PAGES ISSUES SEPARATELY

Dacey, J. (1994). Management participation in corporate buy-outs. <u>Management Perspectives,
7</u>(4), 20-31.

13. AN ARTICLE IN A MAGAZINE

Van Gelder, L. (1986, December). Countdown to
motherhood: When should you have a baby? <u>Ms.,</u>
37-39.

14. AN ARTICLE IN A NEWSPAPER

Ramirez, A. (1993, December 14). Computer groups
plan standards. <u>The New York Times,</u> p. D5.

15. AN UNSIGNED ARTICLE

The right to die. (1976, October 11). <u>Time, 121,</u> 101.

16. A REVIEW

Dinnage, R. (1987, November 29). Against the master and his men [Review of the book <u>A mind of
her own: The life of Karen Horney</u>]. <u>The New
York Times Book Review,</u> 10-11.

Other sources

17. A REPORT

Gerald, K. (1958). <u>Micro-moral problems in obstet-
ric care</u> (Report No. NP-71). St. Louis:
Catholic Hospital Association.

18. AN INFORMATION SERVICE

Jolson, M. K. (1981). <u>Music education for
preschoolers.</u> New York: Teachers College, Columbia University. (ERIC Document Reproduc-
tion Service No. ED 264 488)

40b

19. A GOVERNMENT DOCUMENT

United States Commission on Civil Rights. (1983).

    Greater Baltimore commitment. Washington, DC:

    Author.

20. AN INTERVIEW

Brisick, W. C. (1988, July 1). [Interview with

    Ishmael Reed]. Publishers Weekly, 41-42.

21. A VIDEOTAPE, RECORDING, PERFORMANCE, OR OTHER AUDIO-VISUAL SOURCE

Spielberg, S. (Director). (1993). Schindler's list

    [Videotape]. Los Angeles: Viacom.

Ozawa, S. (Conductor). (1991, April 25). Boston

    Symphony Orchestra concert. Symphony Hall,

    Boston.

22. COMPUTER SOFTWARE OR A SOURCE ON CD-ROM

Project scheduler 8000 [Computer software].

    (1995). Orlando, FL: Scitor.

Willard, B. L. (1992). Changes in occupational

    safety standards, 1970-1990 [CD-ROM]. Ab-

    stract from: UMI-ProQuest File: Dissertation

    Abstracts Item: 7770763

40b

23. AN ONLINE SOURCE

    These models are adapted from both the APA *Publication Manual* and *Electronic Style: A Guide to Citing Electronic Information,* by Xia Li and Nancy B. Crane (1993), which adapts APA style to a range of electronic sources. For personal electronic mail and computer bulletin boards and conferences, APA style requires citing the source in your text in parentheses—for instance, "(G. M. Shay, personal communication, June 6, 1996)."

Article in an online journal:

Palfrey, A. (1996, January). Choice of mates in

```
identical twins [12 paragraphs]. Modern Psy-
chology [Online serial],4(1). Available:
http://www.liasu.edu/modpsy/palfrey4(1).htm
```

Source on a network such as FTP (File Transfer Protocol):

```
Mathews, S. (1995). Architecture in the age of
hyperreality [Online]. Available FTP:
zeus.kent.edu Directory: architecture/
archives File: v2.06
```

Source on the World Wide Web (WWW):

```
Leppik, P. (1996, January 21). The two rules of
Internet security [Online]. Available:
http://www.thinck.com/insec.html
```

NOTE With electronic addresses (following "Available" in the references above), omit any punctuation that is not part of the address, including the period that would fall at the end of the reference.

41
CBE DOCUMENTATION STYLE

Writers in the life sciences, physical sciences, and mathematics rely for documentation style on *Scientific Style and Format: The CBE Style Manual for Authors, Editors, and Publishers,* 6th edition (1994). (CBE is the Council of Biology Editors.) This book details two documentation styles: one very close to APA style, using authors' names and publication dates in parenthetical text citations (see the previous chapter); and one using in-text numbers to refer to a list of numbered references that are sequenced in order of their citation in the text. The latter style is discussed below. Ask your instructor which style you should use.

41a. CBE numbered text citations

In the following examples of CBE in-text citations, the numbers refer to a numbered list of references at the end of the paper:

Two standard references[1,2] use this term.

These forms of immunity have been extensively re-
searched.[3]

According to one report,[4] research into some forms
of viral immunity is almost nonexistent.

Hepburn and Tatin[2] do not discuss this project.

- Within the text, use a raised number or numbers to refer to numbered sources in the reference list at the end
  of the text.
- The number for each source is based on the order in
  which you cite the source in the text: the first cited
  source is 1, the second is 2, and so on.
- When you cite a source you have already cited and
  numbered, use the original number again (see the last
  example above, which reuses the number 2 from the
  first example). This reuse is the key difference between
  the CBE numbered citations and numbered references
  to footnotes or endnotes (pp. 118–20). In the CBE style,
  each source has only one number, determined by the
  order in which the source is cited. With notes, in contrast, the numbering proceeds in sequence, so that
  sources have as many numbers as they have citations
  in the text.
- When you cite two or more sources at once, arrange
  their numbers in sequence and separate them with a
  comma and no space, as in the first example above.

41b

41b. CBE numbered references

Begin the list of sources for the CBE style at the end of
the text, numbering the pages in sequence with the text
pages. Use the page format given for APA references on
page 128 (but you may omit the shortened title before the
page number). For the references themselves, follow these
guidelines:

- Title the list of sources "References."
- Single-space the entries, and double-space between
  entries.
- Arrange the entries in numerical order—that is, in order of their citation in the text, *not* alphabetically.

- Begin each entry on a new line and number it. Type the number on the line of type (not raised), and follow it with a period and a space. Indent subsequent lines of each entry directly under the first word of the first line.
- List authors' names with the last name first, followed by initials for first and middle names. Do not use a comma after the last name or periods or space with the initials.
- Separate authors' names with commas.
- Do not underline or use quotation marks for any titles.
- In journal titles, capitalize all significant words. In book and article titles, capitalize only the first word and any proper nouns.
- For books, separate the name of the publisher from the date of publication with a semicolon and a space. End the reference with the total number of pages in the book, followed by *p.*
- For a journal article, put the date of publication immediately after the title of the journal, followed by the volume number and the inclusive page numbers for the article (with duplicated digits omitted): "Science 1990; 256:212–6." For a journal that pages each issue separately, add the month (and day, if relevant) after the year, and add the issue number in unspaced parentheses after the volume number: "1996 3 Mar;16(8):16." For all journals, use no punctuation between title and date of publication. Put an unspaced semicolon between the date and volume number. Put an unspaced colon between the volume number (or parenthetical issue number) and the inclusive pages (see the examples above and models 6–7).

Books

1. A BOOK WITH ONE AUTHOR

1. Gould SJ. Time's arrow, time's cycle. Cambridge: Harvard Univ Pr; 1987. 222 p.

2. A BOOK WITH MORE THAN ONE AUTHOR

2. Hepburn PX, Tatin JM. Human physiology. New York: Columbia Univ Pr; 1975. 1026 p.

3. A BOOK WITH AN EDITOR

3. Jonson P, editor. Anatomy yearbook. Los Angeles: Anatco; 1987. 628 p.

Index to CBE References

BOOKS
1. A book with one author *136*
2. A book with more than one author *136*
3. A book with an editor *136*
4. A selection from a book *137*
5. An anonymous work *137*

PERIODICALS
6. An article in a journal with continuous pagination throughout the annual volume *137*
7. An article in a journal that pages issues separately *137*
8. An article in a newspaper *138*
9. An article in a magazine *138*

OTHER SOURCES
10. A government document *138*
11. An electronic source *138*

4. A SELECTION FROM A BOOK

4. Krigel R, Laubenstein L, Muggia F. Kaposi's sarcoma. In: Ebbeson P, Biggar RS, Melbye M, editors. AIDS: a basic guide for clinicians. Philadelphia: WB Saunders; 1987. p 100-26.

41b

5. AN ANONYMOUS WORK

5. [Anonymous]. Health care for multiple sclerosis. New York: US Health Care; 1992. 86 p.

Periodicals: Journals, magazines, newspapers

6. AN ARTICLE IN A JOURNAL WITH CONTINUOUS PAGINATION THROUGHOUT THE ANNUAL VOLUME

6. Ancino R, Carter KV, Elwin DJ. Factors contributing to viral immunity: a review of the research. Developmental Biology 1983;30:156-9.

7. AN ARTICLE IN A JOURNAL THAT PAGES ISSUES SEPARATELY

7. Milbank Symposium. Medical decision making for the dying. Milbank Quarterly 1986 Feb;64(2):26-40.

8. AN ARTICLE IN A NEWSPAPER

8. Krauthammer C. Lifeboat ethics: the case of Baby Jesse. Washington Post 1986 June 13;Sect A:33(col 1).

9. AN ARTICLE IN A MAGAZINE

9. Van Gelder L. Countdown to motherhood: when should you have a baby? Ms. 1986 Dec:37-39.

Other sources

10. A GOVERNMENT DOCUMENT

10. House (US). Medicare payment for outpatient occupational therapy services. 102nd Cong., 1st Sess. House Doc. nr 409; 1991.

11. AN ELECTRONIC SOURCE

11. Project scheduler 8000 [computer program]. Version 3.1. Orlando (FL): Scitor; 1995. 1 computer disk: 3 1/2 in. Accompanied by: 1 manual. System requirements: IBM PC or fully compatible computer; DOS 5.0 or higher; 320K RAM; hard disk with a minimum of 2 MB of free space.

12. Grady GF. The here and now of hepatitis B immunization. Today's Medicine [serial online] 1993 May 2;Doc nr 2:[2620 words]. Available from: Public Access Computer Systems Forum PACS-L via Internet. Accessed 1996 Jan 21.

41b

GLOSSARY OF USAGE

This glossary provides notes on words or phrases that often cause problems for writers. The recommendations for standard written English are based on current dictionaries and usage guides. Items labeled NONSTANDARD should be avoided in final drafts of academic and business writing. Those labeled COLLOQUIAL and SLANG appear in some informal writing and may occasionally be used for effect in more formal academic and career writing. (Words and phrases labeled *colloquial* include those labeled *informal* by many dictionaries.) See Chapter 12 for more on levels of language.

a, an   Use *a* before words beginning with consonant sounds: *a historian, a one-o'clock class, a university*. Use *an* before words that begin with vowel sounds, including silent *h*'s: *an orgy, an L, an honor*.

The article before an abbreviation depends on how the abbreviation is read: *She was once an AEC aide* (*AEC* is read as three separate letters); *Many Americans opposed a SALT treaty* (*SALT* is read as one word, *salt*).

See also pp. 42–44 on the uses of *a/an* versus *the*.

accept, except   *Accept* is a verb° meaning "receive." *Except* is usually a preposition° or conjunction° meaning "but for" or "other than"; when it is used as a verb, it means "leave out." *I can accept all your suggestions except the last one. I'm sorry you excepted my last suggestion from your list.*

advice, advise   *Advice* is a noun,° and *advise* is a verb:° *Take my advice; do as I advise you.*

affect, effect   Usually *affect* is a verb,° meaning "to influence," and *effect* is a noun, meaning "result": *The drug did not affect his driving; in fact, it seemed to have no effect at all.* But *effect* occasionally is used as a verb meaning "to bring about": *Her efforts effected a change.* And *affect* is used in psychology as a noun meaning "feeling or emotion": *One can infer much about affect from behavior.*

all ready, already   *All ready* means "completely prepared," and *already* means "by now" or "before now": *We were all ready to go to the movie, but it had already started.*

all right   *All right* is always two words. *Alright* is a common misspelling.

USAGE

all together, altogether *All together* means "in unison," or "gathered in one place." *Altogether* means "entirely." *It's not altogether true that our family never spends vacations all together.*

allusion, illusion An *allusion* is an indirect reference, and an *illusion* is a deceptive appearance: *Paul's constant allusions to Shakespeare created the illusion that he was an intellectual.*

a lot *A lot* is always two words, used informally to mean "many." *Alot* is a common misspelling.

among, between In general, use *between* only for relationships of two and *among* for more than two.

amount, number Use *amount* with a singular noun that names something not countable (a noncount noun°): *The amount of food varies.* Use *number* with a plural noun that names more than one of something countable (a count noun°): *The number of calories must stay the same.*

and/or *And/or* indicates three options: one or the other or both (*The decision is made by the mayor and/or the council*). If you mean all three options, *and/or* is appropriate. Otherwise, use *and* if you mean both, *or* if you mean either.

anxious, eager *Anxious* means "nervous" or "worried" and is usually followed by *about*. *Eager* means "looking forward" and is usually followed by *to*. *I've been anxious about getting blisters. I'm eager* (not *anxious*) *to get new cross-training shoes.*

anybody, any body; anyone, any one *Anybody* and *anyone* are indefinite pronouns;° *any body* is a noun° modified by *any; any one* is a pronoun° or adjective° modified by *any*. *How can anybody communicate with any body of government? Can anyone help Amy? She has more work than any one person can handle.*

any more, anymore *Any more* means "no more"; *anymore* means "now." Both are used in negative constructions: *He doesn't want any more. She doesn't live here anymore.*

anyways, anywheres Nonstandard for *anyway* and *anywhere*.

are, is Use *are* with a plural subject° (*books are*), *is* with a singular subject (*book is*). See pp. 27–30.

as Substituting for *because, since,* or *while, as* may be vague or ambiguous: *As we were stopping to rest, we decided to eat lunch.* (Does *as* mean "while" or "because"?) *As* never should be used as a substitute for *whether* or *who. I'm not sure whether* (not *as*) *we can make it. That's the man who* (not *as*) *gave me directions.*

as, like   See *like, as.*

at this point in time   Wordy for *now, at this point,* or *at this time.*

awful, awfully   Strictly speaking, *awful* means "awe-inspiring." As intensifiers meaning "very" or "extremely" (*He tried awfully hard*), *awful* and *awfully* should be avoided in formal speech or writing.

a while, awhile   *Awhile* is an adverb;° *a while* is an article° and a noun.° *I will be gone awhile* (not *a while*). *I will be gone for a while* (not *awhile*).

bad, badly   In formal speech and writing, *bad* should be used only as an adjective;° the adverb° is *badly. He felt bad because his tooth ached badly.* In *He felt bad,* the verb *felt* is a linking verb° and the adjective *bad* modifies the subject° *he,* not the verb *felt.*

being as, being that   Colloquial for *because,* the preferable word in formal speech or writing: *Because* (not *Being as*) *the world is round, Columbus never did fall off the edge.*

beside, besides   *Beside* is a preposition° meaning "next to." *Besides* is a preposition meaning "except" or "in addition to" as well as an adverb° meaning "in addition." *Besides, several other people besides you want to sit beside Dr. Christensen.*

between, among   See *among, between.*

bring, take   Use *bring* only for movement from a farther place to a nearer one and *take* for any other movement. *First, take these books to the library for renewal, then take them to Mr. Daniels. Bring them back to me when he's finished.*

can, may   Strictly, *can* indicates capacity or ability, and *may* indicates permission: *If I may talk with you a moment, I believe I can solve your problem.*

climatic, climactic   *Climatic* comes from *climate* and refers to weather: *Last winter's temperatures may indicate a climatic change. Climactic* comes from *climax* and refers to a dramatic high point: *During the climactic duel between Hamlet and Laertes, Gertrude drinks poisoned wine.*

complement, compliment   To *complement* something is to add to, complete, or reinforce it: *Her yellow blouse complemented her black hair.* To *compliment* something is to make a flattering remark about it: *He complimented her on her hair.* *Complimentary* can also mean "free": *complimentary tickets.*

conscience, conscious   *Conscience* is a noun° meaning "a sense of right and wrong"; *conscious* is an adjective° meaning "aware" or "awake." *Though I was barely conscious, my conscience nagged me.*

continual, continuous   *Continual* means "constantly recurring": *Most movies on television are continually interrupted by commercials.* *Continuous* means "unceasing": *Some cable channels present movies continuously without commercials.*

could of   See *have, of.*

criteria   The plural of *criterion* (meaning "standard for judgment"): *Our criteria are strict. The most important criterion is a sense of humor.*

data   The plural of *datum* (meaning "fact"). Though *data* is often used as a singular noun, most careful writers still treat it as plural: *The data fail* (not *fails*) *to support the hypothesis.*

device, devise   *Device* is the noun,° and *devise* is the verb:° *Can you devise some device for getting his attention?*

different from, different than   *Different from* is preferred: *His purpose is different from mine.* But *different than* is widely accepted when a construction using *from* would be wordy: *I'm a different person now than I used to be* is preferable to *I'm a different person now from the person I used to be.*

disinterested, uninterested   *Disinterested* means "impartial": *We chose Pete, as a disinterested third party, to decide who was right.* *Uninterested* means "bored" or "lacking interest": *Unfortunately, Pete was completely uninterested in the question.*

don't   *Don't* is the contraction for *do not,* not for *does not: I don't care, you don't care,* and *he doesn't* (not *don't*) *care.*

due to   *Due to* is always acceptable after a verb to refer back to the subject:° *His gray hairs were due to age.* Many object to *due to* meaning "because of" (*Due to the holiday, class was canceled*). A rule of thumb is that *due to* is always correct after a form of the verb *be* but questionable otherwise.

eager, anxious   See *anxious, eager.*

effect   See *affect, effect.*

elicit, illicit   *Elicit* is a verb° meaning "bring out" or "call forth." *Illicit* is an adjective° meaning "unlawful." *The crime elicited an outcry against illicit drugs.*

enthused   Sometimes used colloquially as an adjective° meaning "showing enthusiasm." The preferred adjective is *enthusiastic: The coach was enthusiastic* (not *enthused*) *about the team's victory.*

etc.   *Etc.,* the Latin abbreviation for "and other things," should be avoided in formal writing and should not be used to refer to people. When used, it should not substitute for precision, as in *The government provides health care, etc.,* and it should not end a list beginning *such as* or *for example.*

everybody, every body; everyone, every one   *Everybody* and *everyone* are indefinite pronouns:° *Everybody* (*everyone*) *knows Tom steals. Every one* is a pronoun° modified by *every,* and *every body* a noun° modified by *every.* Both refer to each thing or person of a specific group and are typically followed by *of: The game commissioner has stocked every body of fresh water in the state with fish, and now every one of our rivers is a potential trout stream.*

everyday, every day   *Everyday* is an adjective° meaning "used daily" or "common"; *every day* is a noun° modified by *every: Everyday problems tend to arise every day.*

everywheres   Nonstandard for *everywhere.*

except   See *accept, except.*

explicit, implicit   *Explicit* means "stated outright": *I left explicit instructions. Implicit* means "implied, unstated": *We had an implicit understanding.*

farther, further   *Farther* refers to additional distance (*How much farther is it to the beach?*), and *further* refers to additional time, amount, or other abstract matters (*I don't want to discuss this any further*).

feel   Avoid this word in place of *think* or *believe: She thinks* (not *feels*) *that the law should be changed.*

fewer, less   *Fewer* refers to individual countable items (a plural noun°), *less* to general amounts (a singular noun): *Skim milk has fewer calories than whole milk. We have less milk left than I thought.*

further   See *farther, further.*

get *Get* is easy to overuse; watch out for it in expressions such as *it's getting better* (substitute *improving*), *we got done* (substitute *finished*), and *the mayor has got to* (substitute *must*).

good, well *Good* is an adjective,° and *well* is nearly always an adverb:° *Larry's a good dancer. He and Linda dance well together. Well* is properly used as an adjective only to refer to health: *You look well.* (*You look good,* in contrast, means "Your appearance is pleasing.")

hanged, hung Though both are past-tense forms° of *hang, hanged* is used to refer to executions and *hung* is used for all other meanings: *Tom Dooley was hanged* (not *hung*) *from a white oak tree. I hung* (not *hanged*) *the picture you gave me.*

have, of Use *have*, not *of*, after helping verbs° such as *could, should, would, may*, and *might: You should have* (not *should of*) *told me.*

he, she; he/she Convention has allowed the use of *he* to mean "he or she," but most writers today consider this usage inaccurate and unfair because it excludes females. The construction *he/she*, one substitute for *he*, is awkward and objectionable to most readers. The better choice is to use *he or she*, to recast the sentence in the plural, or to rephrase. For instance: *After the infant learns to creep, he or she progresses to crawling. After infants learn to creep, they progress to crawling. After learning to creep, the infant progresses to crawling.* See also pp. 10–11 and 36–37.

herself, himself See *myself, herself, himself, yourself.*

hisself Nonstandard for *himself.*

hopefully *Hopefully* means "with hope": *Freddy waited hopefully.* The use of *hopefully* to mean "it is to be hoped," "I hope," or "let's hope" is now very common; but since many readers continue to object strongly to the usage, you should avoid it. *I hope* (not *Hopefully*) *Eliza will be here soon.*

if, whether For clarity, use *whether* rather than *if* when you are expressing an alternative: *If I laugh hard, people can't tell whether I'm crying.*

illicit See *elicit, illicit.*

illusion See *allusion, illusion.*

implicit See *explicit, implicit.*

imply, infer   Writers or speakers *imply*, meaning "suggest": *Jim's letter implies he's having a good time.* Readers or listeners *infer*, meaning "conclude": *From Jim's letter I infer he's having a good time.*

irregardless   Nonstandard for *regardless*.

is, are   See *are, is.*

is when, is where   These are faulty constructions in sentences that define: *Adolescence is a stage* (not *is when a person is*) *between childhood and adulthood. Socialism is a system in which* (not *is where*) *government owns the means of production.*

its, it's   *Its* is the pronoun° *it* in the possessive case:° *That plant is losing its leaves. It's* is a contraction for *it is: It's likely to die if you don't water it.*

kind of, sort of, type of   In formal speech and writing, avoid using *kind of* or *sort of* to mean "somewhat": *He was rather* (not *kind of*) *tall.*

   Kind, sort, and *type* are singular: *This kind of dog is easily trained.* Errors often occur when these singular nouns are combined with the plural adjectives° *these* and *those: These kinds* (not *kind*) *of dogs are easily trained. Kind, sort,* and *type* should be followed by *of* but not by *a: I don't know what type of* (not *type* or *type of a*) *dog that is.*

   Use *kind of, sort of,* or *type of* only when the word *kind, sort,* or *type* is important: *That was a strange* (not *strange sort of*) *statement.*

lay, lie   *Lay* means "put" or "place" and takes a direct object:° *We could lay the tablecloth in the sun.* Its main forms are *lay, laid, laid. Lie* means "recline" or "be situated" and does not take an object: *I lie awake at night. The town lies east of the river.* Its main forms are *lie, lay, lain.*

less   See *fewer, less.*

lie, lay   See *lay, lie.*

like, as   In formal speech and writing, *like* should not introduce a full clause.° The preferred choice is *as* or *as if: The plan succeeded as* (not *like*) *we hoped.* Use *like* only before a word or phrase: *Other plans like it have failed.*

literally   This word means "actually" or "just as the words say," and it should not be used to intensify expressions whose words are not to be taken at face value. The sentence *He was literally climbing the walls* describes a person behav-

USAGE

ing like an insect, not a person who is restless or anxious. For the latter meaning, *literally* should be omitted.

lose, loose   *Lose* means "mislay": *Did you lose a brown glove? Loose* usually means "unrestrained" or "not tight": *Ann's canary got loose.*

may, can   See *can, may.*

may be, maybe   *May be* is a verb,° and *maybe* is an adverb° meaning "perhaps": *Tuesday may be a legal holiday. Maybe we won't have classes.*

may of   See *have, of.*

media   *Media* is the plural of *medium* and takes a plural verb:° *All the news media are increasingly visual.*

might of   See *have, of.*

must of   See *have, of.*

myself, herself, himself, yourself   The *-self* pronouns° refer to or intensify another word or words: *Paul did it himself; Jill herself said so.* In formal speech or writing, avoid using the *-self* pronouns in place of personal pronouns:° *No one except me* (not *myself*) *saw the accident. Michiko and I* (not *myself*) *planned the ceremony.*

nowheres   Nonstandard for *nowhere.*

number   See *amount, number.*

of, have   See *have, of.*

OK, O.K., okay   All three spellings are acceptable, but avoid this colloquial term in formal speech and writing.

people, persons   Except when emphasizing individuals, prefer *people* to *persons: We the people of the United States . . . ; Will the person or persons who saw the accident please notify. . . .*

percent (per cent), percentage   Both these terms refer to fractions of one hundred. *Percent* always follows a numeral (*40 percent of the voters*), and the word should be used instead of the symbol (%) in nontechnical writing. *Percentage* usually follows an adjective (*a high percentage*).

persons   See *people, persons.*

phenomena   The plural of *phenomenon* (meaning "perceivable fact" or "unusual occurrence"): *Many phenomena are not recorded. One phenomenon is attracting attention.*

plus *Plus* is standard as a preposition° meaning "in addition to": *His income plus mine is sufficient.* But *plus* is colloquial as a conjunctive adverb:° *Our organization is larger than theirs; moreover* (not *plus*), *we have more money.*

precede, proceed *Precede* means "come before": *My name precedes yours in the alphabet. Proceed* means "move on": *We were told to proceed to the waiting room.*

prejudice, prejudiced *Prejudice* is a noun;° *prejudiced* is an adjective.° Do not drop the *-d* from *prejudiced: I was fortunate that my parents were not prejudiced* (not *prejudice*).

principal, principle *Principal* is an adjective° meaning "foremost" or "major," a noun° meaning "chief official," or, in finance, a noun meaning "capital sum." *Principle* is a noun only, meaning "rule" or "axiom." *Her principal reasons for confessing were her principles of right and wrong.*

proceed, precede See *precede, proceed.*

raise, rise *Raise* means "lift" or "bring up" and takes a direct object:° *The Kirks raise cattle.* Its main forms are *raise, raised, raised. Rise* means "get up" and does not take an object: *They must rise at dawn.* Its main forms are *rise, rose, risen.*

real, really In formal speech and writing, *real* should not be used as an adverb;° *really* is the adverb and *real* an adjective.° *Popular reaction to the announcement was really* (not *real*) *enthusiastic.*

reason is because Although colloquially common, this construction should be avoided in formal speech and writing. Use a *that* clause after *reason is: The reason he is absent is that* (not *is because*) *he is sick.* Or: *He is absent because he is sick.*

respectful, respective *Respectful* means "full of (or showing) respect": *Be respectful of other people. Respective* means "separate": *The French and the Germans occupied their respective trenches.*

rise, raise See *raise, rise.*

sensual, sensuous *Sensual* suggests sexuality; *sensuous* means "pleasing to the senses." *Stirred by the sensuous scent of meadow grass and flowers, Cheryl and Paul found their thoughts turning sensual.*

set, sit *Set* means "put" or "place" and takes a direct object:° *He sets the pitcher down.* Its main forms are *set, set, set. Sit* means "be seated" and does not take an object: *She sits on the sofa.* Its main forms are *sit, sat, sat.*

should of   See *have, of.*

since   *Since* mainly relates to time: *I've been waiting since noon.* But *since* is also often used to mean "because": *Since you ask, I'll tell you.* Revise sentences in which the word could have either meaning, such as *Since you left, my life is empty.*

sit, set   See *set, sit.*

somebody, some body; someone, some one   *Somebody* and *someone* are indefinite pronouns;° *some body* is a noun° modified by *some;* and *some one* is a pronoun° or an adjective° modified by *some. Somebody ought to invent a shampoo that will give hair some body. Someone told James he should choose some one plan and stick with it.*

sometime, sometimes, some time   *Sometime* means "at an indefinite time in the future": *Why don't you come up and see me sometime? Sometimes* means "now and then": *I still see my old friend Joe sometimes. Some time* means "span of time": *I need some time to make the payments.*

somewheres   Nonstandard for *somewhere.*

sort of, sort of a   See *kind of, sort of, type of.*

supposed to, used to   In both these expressions, the *-d* is essential: *I used to* (not *use to*) *think so. He's supposed to* (not *suppose to*) *meet us.*

sure and, sure to; try and, try to   *Sure to* and *try to* are the preferred forms: *Be sure to* (not *sure and*) *buy milk. Try to* (not *Try and*) *find some decent tomatoes.*

take, bring   See *bring, take.*

than, then   *Than* is a conjunction° used in comparisons, *then* an adverb° indicating time: *Holmes knew then that Moriarty was wilier than he had thought.*

that, which   *That* always introduces restrictive clauses:° *We should use the lettuce that Susan bought* (*that Susan bought* limits *lettuce* to a particular lettuce). *Which* can introduce both restrictive and nonrestrictive clauses,° but many writers reserve *which* only for nonrestrictive clauses: *The leftover lettuce, which is in the refrigerator, would make a good salad* (*which is in the refrigerator* simply provides more information about the lettuce we already know of). Restrictive clauses (with *that* or *which*) are not set off by commas; nonrestrictive clauses (with *which*) are. See also pp. 54–55.

USAGE

their, there, they're   *Their* is the possessive° form of *they:* *Give them their money.* *There* indicates place (*I saw her standing there*) or functions as an expletive° (*There is a hole behind you*). *They're* is a contraction° for *they are: They're going fast.*

theirselves   Nonstandard for *themselves.*

then, than   See *than, then.*

these kind, these sort, these type, those kind   See *kind of, sort of, type of.*

thru   A colloquial spelling of *through* that should be avoided in all academic and business writing.

to, too, two   *To* is a preposition;° *too* is an adverb° meaning "also" or "excessively"; and *two* is a number. *I too have been to Europe two times.*

toward, towards   Both are acceptable, though *toward* is preferred. Use one or the other consistently.

try and, try to   See *sure and, sure to; try and, try to.*

type of   Don't use *type* without *of: It was a family type of* (not *type*) *restaurant.* Or, better: *It was a family restaurant.* See also *kind of, sort of, type of.*

uninterested   See *disinterested, uninterested.*

unique   *Unique* means "the only one of its kind" and so cannot sensibly by modified with words such as *very* or *most: That was a unique* (not *a very unique* or *the most unique*) *movie.*

used to   See *supposed to, used to.*

wait for, wait on   In formal speech and writing, *wait for* means "await" (*I'm waiting for Paul*), and *wait on* means "serve" (*The owner of the store herself waited on us*).

weather, whether   The *weather* is the state of the atmosphere. *Whether* introduces alternatives. *The weather will determine whether we go or not.*

well   See *good, well.*

whether, if   See *if, whether.*

which, who   *Which* never refers to people. Use *who* or sometimes *that* for a person or persons and *which* or *that* for a thing or things: *The baby, who was left behind, opened the door, which we had closed.*

who's, whose *Who's* is the contraction° of *who is: Who's at the door? Whose* is the possessive° form of *who: Whose book is that?*

would have Avoid this construction in place of *had* in clauses that begin *if* and state a condition contrary to fact: *If the tree had* (not *would have*) *withstood the fire, it would have been the oldest in town.*

would of See *have, of.*

you In all but very formal writing, *you* is generally appropriate as long as it means "you, the reader." In all writing, avoid indefinite uses of *you,* such as *In one ancient tribe your first loyalty was to your parents.*

your, you're *Your* is the possessive° form of *you: Your dinner is ready. You're* is the contraction° of *you are: You're bound to be late.*

yourself See *myself, herself, himself, yourself.*

GLOSSARY OF TERMS

This glossary defines the terms and concepts of basic English grammar, including every term marked ° in the text.

absolute phrase   A phrase that consists of a noun° or pronoun° plus the *-ing* or *-ed* form of a verb° (a participle°): *Our accommodations arranged, we set out on our trip. They will hire a local person, other things being equal.*

active voice   The verb form° used when the sentence subject° names the performer of the verb's action: *The drillers used a rotary blade.* For more, see *voice*.

adjective   A word used to modify a noun° or pronoun:° *beautiful morning, ordinary one, good spelling.* Contrast *adverb*. Nouns, word groups, and some verb° forms may also serve as adjectives: *book sale; sale of old books; the sale, which occurs annually; increasing profits.*

adverb   A word used to modify a verb,° an adjective,° another adverb, or a whole sentence: *warmly greet* (verb), *only three people* (adjective), *quite seriously* (adverb), *Fortunately, she is employed* (sentence). Word groups may also serve as adverbs: *drove by a farm, plowed the fields when the earth thawed.*

agreement   The correspondence of one word to another in person,° number,° or gender.° Mainly, a verb° must agree with its subject° (*The chef orders eggs*), and a pronoun° must agree with it antecedent° (*The chef surveys her breakfast*). See also pp. 27–30 and 35–37.

antecedent   The word a pronoun° refers to: *Jonah, who is not yet ten, has already chosen the college he will attend* (*Jonah* is the antecedent of the pronouns *who* and *he*).

appositive   A word or word group appearing next to a noun° or pronoun° that renames or identifies it and is equivalent to it: *My brother Michael, the best horn player in town, won the state competition* (*Michael* identifies which brother is being referred to; *the best horn player in town* renames *My brother Michael*).

article   The words *a, an,* and *the.* Articles always signal that a noun follows. See p. 139 for how to choose between *a* and *an.* See pp. 42–44 for the rules governing *a/an* and *the.*

auxiliary verb   See *helping verb*.

case The form of a pronoun° or noun° that indicates its function in the sentence. Most pronouns have three cases. The SUBJECTIVE CASE is for subjects° and subject complements:° *I, you, he, she, it, we, they, who, whoever.* The OBJECTIVE CASE is for objects:° *me, you, him, her, it, us, them, whom, whomever.* The POSSESSIVE CASE is for ownership: *my/mine, your/yours, his, her/hers, its, our/ours, their/theirs, whose.* Nouns use the subjective form (*dog, America*) for all cases except the possessive (*dog's, America's*).

clause A group of words containing a subject° and a predicate.° A MAIN CLAUSE can stand alone as a sentence: <u>*We can go to the movies*</u>. A SUBORDINATE CLAUSE cannot stand alone as a sentence: *We can go* <u>*if Julie gets back on time*</u>. For more, see *subordinate clause*.

collective noun A word with singular form that names a group of individuals or things: for instance, *team, army, family, flock, group.* A collective noun generally takes a singular verb and a singular pronoun: *The* <u>*army is*</u> *prepared for* <u>*its*</u> *role.* See also pp. 29 and 37.

comma splice A sentence error in which two sentences (main clauses°) are separated by a comma without *and, but, or, nor,* or another coordinating conjunction.° Splice: *The book was long, it contained useful information.* Revised: *The book was long; it contained useful information.* Or: *The book was long, <u>and</u> it contained useful information.* See pp. 48–50.

comparison The form of an adverb° or adjective° that shows its degree of quality or amount. The POSITIVE is the simple, uncompared form: *gross, clumsily.* The COMPARATIVE compares the thing modified to at least one other thing: *grosser, more clumsily.* The SUPERLATIVE indicates that the thing modified exceeds all other things to which it is being compared: *grossest, most clumsily.* The comparative and superlative are formed either with the endings *-er* and *-est* or with the words *more* and *most* or *less* and *least.*

complement See *subject complement*.

complex sentence See *sentence*.

compound-complex sentence See *sentence*.

compound construction Two or more words or word groups serving the same function, such as a compound subject° (<u>*Harriet and Peter poled their barge down the river*</u>), a compound predicate° (*The scout <u>watched and waited</u>*), or a compound sentence (<u>*He smiled, and I laughed*</u>).

compound sentence   See *sentence*.

conditional statement   A statement expressing a condition contrary to fact and using the subjunctive mood° of the verb: *If she were mayor, the unions would cooperate.*

conjunction   A word that links and relates parts of a sentence. See *coordinating conjunction* (*and, but,* etc.), *correlative conjunction* (*either . . . or, both . . . and,* etc.), and *subordinating conjunction* (*because, if,* etc.).

conjunctive adverb   An adverb° that can relate two complete sentences (main clauses°) in a single sentence: *We had hoped to own a house by now; however, prices are still too high.* The main clauses are separated by a semicolon or a period. Some common conjunctive adverbs: *accordingly, also, anyway, besides, certainly, consequently, finally, further, furthermore, hence, however, incidentally, indeed, instead, likewise, meanwhile, moreover, namely, nevertheless, next, nonetheless, now, otherwise, similarly, still, then, thereafter, therefore, thus, undoubtedly.*

contraction   A condensed expression, with an apostrophe replacing the missing letters: for example, *doesn't* (*does not*), *we'll* (*we will*).

coordinating conjunction   A word linking words or word groups serving the same function: *The dog and cat sometimes fight, but they usually get along.* The coordinating conjunctions are *and, but, or, nor, for, so, yet.*

coordination   The linking of words or word groups that are of equal importance, usually with a coordinating conjunction.° *He and I laughed, but she was not amused.* Contrast *subordination.*

correlative conjunction   Two or more connecting words that work together to link words or word groups serving the same function: *Both Michiko and June signed up, but neither Stan nor Carlos did.* The correlatives include *both . . . and, just as . . . so, not only . . . but also, not . . . but, either . . . or, neither . . . nor, whether . . . or, as . . . as.*

count noun   A word that names a person, place, or thing that can be counted (and so may appear in plural form): *camera/cameras, river/rivers, child/children.*

dangling modifier   A modifier that does not sensibly describe anything in its sentence. Dangling: *Having arrived late, the concert had already begun.* Revised: *Having arrived late, we found that the concert had already begun.* See p. 46.

TERMS

determiner   A word such as *a, an, the, my,* and *your* that indicates that a noun follows. See also *article.*

direct address   A construction in which a word or phrase indicates the person or group spoken to: *Have you finished, John? Farmers, unite.*

direct object   A noun° or pronoun° that identifies who or what receives the action of a verb:° *Education opens doors.* For more, see *object* and *predicate.*

direct question   A sentence asking a question and concluding with a question mark: *Do they know we are watching?* Contrast *indirect question.*

direct quotation   Repetition of what someone has written or said, using the exact words of the original and enclosing them in quotation marks: *Feinberg writes, "The reasons are both obvious and sorry."*

double negative   A nonstandard form consisting of two negative words used in the same construction so that they effectively cancel each other: *I don't have no money.* Rephrase as *I have no money* or *I don't have any money.*

ellipsis   The omission of a word or words from a quotation, indicated by the three spaced periods of an ELLIPSIS MARK: *"that all . . . are created equal."* See also pp. 67–68.

expletive construction   A sentence that postpones the subject° by beginning with *there* or *it* and a form of *be: It is impossible to get a ticket. There are no more seats available.*

first person   See *person.*

fused sentence (run-on sentence)   A sentence error in which two complete sentences (main clauses°) are joined with no punctuation or connecting word between them. Fused: *I heard his lecture it was dull.* Revised: *I heard his lecture; it was dull.* See pp. 48–50.

future perfect tense   The verb tense expressing an action that will be completed before another future action: *They will have heard by then.* For more, see *tense.*

future tense   The verb tense expressing action that will occur in the future: *They will hear soon.* For more, see *tense.*

gender   The classification of nouns° or pronouns° as masculine (*he, boy*), feminine (*she, woman*), or neuter (*it, typewriter*).

TERMS

gerund A verb form that ends in *-ing* and functions as a noun:° *Working is all right for killing time.* For more, see *verbals and verbal phrases.*

gerund phrase See *verbals and verbal phrases.*

helping verb (auxiliary verb) A verb° used with another verb to convey time, possibility, obligation, and other meanings: *You should write a letter. You have written other letters.* The MODALS are the following: *can, could, may, might, must, ought, shall, should, will, would.* The other helping verbs are forms of *be, have,* and *do.*

idiom An expression that is peculiar to a language and that may not make sense if taken literally: for example, *dark horse, bide your time,* and *by and large.*

imperative See *mood.*

indefinite pronoun A word that stands for a noun° and does not refer to a specific person or thing: *all, any, anybody, anyone, anything, each, either, everybody, everyone, everything, neither, nobody, none, no one, nothing, one, some, somebody, someone, something.* Indefinite pronouns usually take singular verbs and are referred to by singular pronouns (*something makes its presence felt*). See also pp. 28, 36–37.

indicative See *mood.*

indirect object A noun° or pronoun° that identifies to whom or what something is done: *Give them the award.* For more, see *object* and *predicate.*

indirect question A sentence reporting a question and ending with a period: *Writers wonder if their work must always be lonely.* Contrast *direct question.*

indirect quotation A report of what someone has written or said, but not using the exact words of the original and not enclosing the words in quotation marks. Quotation: *"Events have controlled me."* Indirect quotation: *Lincoln said that events had controlled him.*

infinitive A verb form° consisting of the verb's dictionary form plus *to: to swim, to write.* For more, see *verbals and verbal phrases.*

infinitive phrase See *verbals and verbal phrases.*

intensive pronoun See *pronoun.*

interjection   A word standing by itself or inserted in a construction to exclaim or command attention: *Hey! Ouch! What the heck did you do that for?*

interrogative pronoun   See *pronoun*.

intransitive verb   A verb° that does not require a following word (direct object°) to complete its meaning: *Mosquitoes buzz. The hospital may close.* For more, see *predicate*.

irregular verb   See *verb forms*.

linking verb   A verb that links, or connects, a subject° and a word that renames or describes the subject (a subject complement°): *They are golfers. You seem lucky.* The linking verbs are the forms of *be*, the verbs of the senses (*look, sound, smell, feel, taste*), and a few others (*appear, become, grow, prove, remain, seem, turn*). For more, see *predicate*.

main clause   A word group that contains a subject° and a predicate,° does not begin with a subordinating word, and may stand alone as a sentence: *The president was not overbearing.* For more, see *clause*.

main verb   The part of a verb phrase° that carries the principal meaning: *had been walking, could happen, was chilled.* Contrast *helping verb*.

misplaced modifier   A modifier so far from the term it modifies or so close to another term it could modify that its relation to the rest of the sentence is unclear. Misplaced: *The children played with firecrackers that they bought illegally in the field.* Revised: *The children played in the field with firecrackers that they bought illegally.*

modal   See *helping verb*.

modifier   Any word or word group that limits or qualifies the meaning of another word or word group. Modifiers include adjectives° and adverbs° as well as words and word groups that act as adjectives and adverbs.

mood   The form of a verb° that shows how the speaker views the action. The INDICATIVE MOOD, the most common, is used to make statements or ask questions: *The play will be performed Saturday. Did you get tickets?* The IMPERATIVE MOOD gives a command: *Please get good seats. Avoid the top balcony.* The SUBJUNCTIVE MOOD expresses a wish, a condition contrary to fact, a recommendation, or a request: *I wish George were coming with us. If he were here, he'd come.*

noncount noun   A word that names a person, place, or thing and that is not considered countable in English (and so does not appear in plural form): *confidence, information, silver, work.*

nonrestrictive clause   See *nonrestrictive element.*

nonrestrictive element   A word or word group that does not limit the word it refers to and that is not essential to the meaning of the sentence. Nonrestrictive elements are usually set off by commas: *Sleep, which we all need, occupies a third of our lives. His wife, Patricia, is a chemist.* Contrast *restrictive element.*

noun   A word that names a person, place, thing, quality, or idea: *Maggie, Alabama, clarinet, satisfaction, socialism.* See also *collective noun, count noun, noncount noun,* and *proper noun.*

noun clause   See *subordinate clause.*

number   The form of a word that indicates whether it is singular or plural. Singular: *I, he, this, child, runs, hides.* Plural: *we, they, these, children, run, hide.*

object   A noun° or pronoun° that receives the action of or is influenced by another word. A DIRECT OBJECT receives the action of a verb° or verbal° and usually follows it in a sentence: *We watched the stars.* An INDIRECT OBJECT tells for or to whom something is done: *Reiner bought us tapes.* An OBJECT OF A PREPOSITION usually follows a preposition° and is linked by it to the rest of the sentence: *They are going to New Orleans for the jazz festival.*

objective case   The form of a pronoun° when it is the object° of a verb° (*call him*) or the object of a preposition° (*for us*). For more, see *case.*

object of preposition   See *object.*

parallelism   Similarity of grammatical form between two or more coordinated elements: *Rising prices and declining incomes left many people in bad debt and worse despair.* See pp. 4–5.

parenthetical expression   A word or construction that interrupts a sentence and is not part of its main structure, called *parenthetical* because it could (or does) appear in parentheses: *Mary Cassatt (1845–1926) was an American painter. Her work, incidentally, is in the museum.*

TERMS

participial phrase See *verbals and verbal phrases*.

participle See *verbals and verbal phrases*.

particle A preposition° or adverb° in a two-word verb: *catch on, look up*.

parts of speech The classes into which words are commonly grouped according to their form, function, and meaning: nouns, pronouns, verbs, adjectives, adverbs, conjunctions, prepositions, and interjections. See separate entries for each part of speech.

passive voice The verb form° used when the sentence subject° names the receiver of the verb's action: *The mixture was stirred*. For more, see *voice*.

past participle The *-ed* form of most verbs:° *fished, hopped*. Some verbs form their past participles in irregular ways: *begun, written*. For more, see *verbals and verbal phrases* and *verb forms*.

past perfect tense The verb tense expressing an action that was completed before another past action: *No one had heard that before*. For more, see *tense*.

past tense The verb tense expressing action that occurred in the past: *Everyone laughed*. For more, see *tense*.

past-tense form The verb form used to indicate action that occurred in the past, usually created by adding *-d* or *-ed* to the verb's dictionary form (*smiled*) but created differently for most irregular verbs (*began, threw*). For more, see *verb forms*.

perfect tenses The verb tenses indicating action completed before another specific time or action: *have walked, had walked, will have walked*. For more, see *tense*.

person The form of a verb° or pronoun° that indicates whether the subject is speaking, spoken to, or spoken about. In the FIRST PERSON the subject is speaking: *I am, we are*. In the SECOND PERSON the subject is spoken to: *you are*. In the THIRD PERSON the subject is spoken about: *he/she/it is, they are*.

personal pronoun *I, you, he, she, it, we*, or *they:* a word that substitutes for a specific noun° or other pronoun. For more, see *case*.

phrase A group of related words that lacks a subject° or a predicate° or both: *She ran into the field. She tried to jump the fence*. See also *absolute phrase, prepositional phrase, verbals and verbal phrases*.

plain form The dictionary form of a verb: *buy, make, run, swivel*. For more, see *verb forms*.

plural More than one. See *number*.

positive form See *comparison*.

possessive case The form of a noun° or pronoun° that indicates its ownership of something else: *men's attire, your briefcase*. For more, see *case*.

predicate The part of a sentence that makes an assertion about the subject.° The predicate may consist of an intransitive verb° (*The earth trembled*), a transitive verb° plus direct object° (*The earthquake shook buildings*), a linking verb° plus subject complement° (*The result was chaos*), a transitive verb plus indirect object° and direct object (*The government sent the city aid*), or a transitive verb plus direct object and object complement (*The citizens considered the earthquake a disaster*).

preposition A word that forms a noun° or pronoun° (plus any modifiers) into a PREPOSITIONAL PHRASE: *about love, down the steep stairs*. The common prepositions: *about, above, according to, across, after, against, along, along with, among, around, as, at, because of, before, behind, below, beneath, beside, between, beyond, by, concerning, despite, down, during, except, except for, excepting, for, from, in, in addition to, inside, in spite of, instead of, into, like, near, next to, of, off, on, onto, out, out of, outside, over, past, regarding, since, through, throughout, till, to, toward, under, underneath, unlike, until, up, upon, with, within, without*.

prepositional phrase A word group consisting of a preposition° and its object.° Prepositional phrases usually serve as adjectives° (*We saw a movie about sorrow*) and as adverbs° (*We went back for the second show*).

present participle The *-ing* form of a verb:° *swimming, flying*. For more, see *verbals and verbal phrases*.

present perfect tense The verb tense expressing action that began in the past and is linked to the present: *Dogs have buried bones here before*. For more, see *tense*.

present tense The verb tense expressing action that is occurring now, occurs habitually, or is generally true: *Dogs bury bones here often*. For more, see *tense*.

principal parts The three forms of a verb from which its various tenses are created: the PLAIN FORM (*stop, go*), the PAST-TENSE FORM (*stopped, went*), and the PAST PARTICIPLE (*stopped, gone*). For more, see *tense* and *verb forms*.

TERMS

progressive tenses   The verb tenses that indicate continuing (progressive) action and use the *-ing* form of the verb: *A dog was burying a bone here this morning.* For more, see *tense.*

pronoun   A word used in place of a noun,° such as *I, he, everyone, who,* and *herself.* See also *indefinite pronoun, personal pronoun, relative pronoun.*

proper noun   A word naming a specific person, place, or thing and beginning with a capital letter: *David Letterman, Mt. Rainier, Washington, U.S. Congress.*

regular verb   See *verb forms.*

relative pronoun   *Who, whoever, which,* or *that:* a word that relates a group of words to a noun° or other pronoun:° *Ask the woman who knows all. This may be the question that stumps her.* For more, see *case.*

restrictive clause   See *restrictive element.*

restrictive element   A word or word group that is essential to the meaning of the sentence because it limits the word it refers to: removing it would leave the meaning unclear or too general. Restrictive elements are *not* set off by commas: *Dorothy's companion the Scarecrow lacks a brain. The man who called about the apartment said he'd try again.* Contrast *nonrestrictive element.*

run-on sentence   See *fused sentence.*

-s form   See *verb forms.*

second person   See *person.*

sentence   A complete unit of thought, consisting of at least a subject° and a predicate° that are not introduced by a subordinating word. Sentences can be classed on the basis of their structure: A SIMPLE SENTENCE contains one main clause:° *I'm leaving.* A COMPOUND SENTENCE contains at least two main clauses: *I'd like to stay, but I'm leaving.* A COMPLEX SENTENCE contains one main clause and at least one subordinate clause:° *If you let me go now, you'll be sorry.* A COMPOUND-COMPLEX SENTENCE contains at least two main clauses and at least one subordinate clause: *I'm leaving because you want me to, but I'd rather stay.*

sentence fragment   A sentence error in which a group of words is set off as a sentence even though it begins with a subordinating word or lacks a subject° or a predicate° or both. Fragment: *She was not in shape for the race. Which she* *had hoped to win*. Revised: *She was not in shape for the race, which she had hoped to win*. See pp. 47–48.

series Three or more items with the same function: *We gorged on ham, eggs, and potatoes*.

simple sentence See *sentence*.

simple tenses See *tense*.

singular One. See *number*.

split infinitive The usually awkward interruption of an infinitive° and its marker *to* by a modifier: *Management decided to not introduce the new product*. See p. 45.

squinting modifier A modifier that could modify the words on either side of it: *The plan we considered seriously worries me*.

subject In grammar, the part of a sentence that names something and about which an assertion is made in the predicate:° *The quick, brown fox jumped lazily* (simple subject); *The quick, brown fox jumped lazily* (complete subject).

subject complement A word that renames or describes the subject° of a sentence, after a linking verb:° *The stranger was a man* (noun°). *He seemed gigantic* (adjective°).

subjective case The form of a pronoun° when it is the subject° of a sentence (*I called*) or a subject complement° (*It was I*). For more, see *case*.

subjunctive See *mood*.

subordinate clause A word group that consists of a subject° and a predicate,° begins with a subordinating word such as *because* or *who*, and is not a question: *They voted for whoever seemed to care the least because they mistrusted politicians*. Subordinate clauses may serve as adjectives° (*The car that hit Fred was running a red light*), as adverbs° (*The car hit Fred when it ran a red light*), or as nouns° (*Whoever was driving should be arrested*). Subordinate clauses may *not* serve as complete sentences.

subordinating conjunction A word that forms a complete sentence into a word group (a subordinate clause°) that can serve as an adverb° or a noun.° *Everyone was relieved when the meeting ended*. Some common subordinating conjunctions: *after, although, as, as if, as long as, as though, because, before, even if, even though, if, if only, in order that, now that, once, rather than, since, so that, than, that, though, till, unless, until, when, whenever, where, whereas, wherever, while*.

TERMS

subordination The use of grammatical structures to de-emphasize one element in a sentence by making it dependent on rather than equal to another element. Through subordination, *I left six messages; the doctor failed to call* becomes *Although I left six messages, the doctor failed to call* or *After six messages, the doctor failed to call.*

tag question A question attached to the end of a statement and composed of a pronoun,° a helping verb,° and sometimes the word *not: It isn't raining, is it? It is sunny, isn't it?*

tense The form of a verb° that expresses the time of its action, usually indicated by the verb's endings and by helping verbs. See also *verb forms.*

PRESENT   Action that is occurring now, occurs habitually, or is generally true

SIMPLE PRESENT Plain form or -s form	PRESENT PROGRESSIVE *Am, is,* or *are* plus -ing form
I *walk.*	I *am walking.*
You/we/they *walk.*	You/we/they *are walking.*
He/she/it *walks.*	He/she/it *is walking.*

PAST   Action that occurred before now

SIMPLE PAST Past-tense form (-d or -ed)	PAST PROGRESSIVE *Was* or *were* plus -ing form
I/he/she/it *walked.*	I/he/she/it *was walking.*
You/we/they *walked.*	You/we/they *were walking.*

FUTURE   Action that will occur in the future

SIMPLE FUTURE *Will* plus plain form	FUTURE PROGRESSIVE *Will be* plus -ing form
I/you/he/she/it/we/they *will walk.*	I/you/he/she/it/we/they *will be walking.*

PRESENT PERFECT   Action that began in the past and is linked to the present

PRESENT PERFECT *Have* or *has* plus past participle (-d or -ed)	PRESENT PERFECT PROGRESSIVE *Have been* or *has been* plus -ing form
I/you/we/they *have walked.*	I/you/we/they *have been walking.*
He/she/it *has walked.*	He/she/it *has been walking.*

PAST PERFECT   Action that was completed before another past action

PAST PERFECT *Had* plus past participle (-d or -ed)	PAST PERFECT PROGRESSIVE *Had been* plus -ing form

| I/you/he/she/it/we/they *had walked.* | I/you/he/she/it/we/they *had been walking.* |

FUTURE PERFECT   Action that will be completed before another future action

| FUTURE PERFECT   *Will have* plus past participle (*-d* or *-ed*) | FUTURE PERFECT PROGRESSIVE   *Will have been* plus *-ing* form |
| I/you/he/she/it/we/they *will have walked.* | I/you/he/she/it/we/they *will have been walking.* |

transitional expression   A word or phrase that links sentences and shows the relations between them. Transitional expressions can signal the following: addition or sequence (*also, besides, finally, first, furthermore, in addition, last*); comparison (*also, likewise, similarly*); contrast (*even so, however, in contrast, nevertheless, still*); examples (*for example, for instance, specifically, that is*); intensification (*indeed, in fact, of course, truly*); place (*below, elsewhere, here, nearby, to the east*); time (*afterward, at last, earlier, immediately, meanwhile, shortly, simultaneously*); repetition or summary (*all in all, in brief, in other words, in short, in summary, that is*); and cause and effect (*as a result, consequently, hence, otherwise, therefore, thus*).

transitive verb   A verb° that requires a following word (a direct object°) to complete its meaning: *We <u>raised</u> the roof.* For more, see *predicate*.

verb   A word that expresses an action (*bring, change*), an occurrence (*happen, become*), or a state of being (*be, seem*). A verb is the essential word in a predicate,° the part of a sentence that makes an assertion about the subject.° With endings and helping verbs,° verbs can indicate tense,° mood,° voice,° number,° and person.° For more, see separate entries for each of these aspects as well as *verb forms*.

verbals and verbal phrases   VERBALS are verb forms used as adjectives,° adverbs,° or nouns.° They form VERBAL PHRASES with objects° and modifiers. A PRESENT PARTICIPLE adds *-ing* to the dictionary form of a verb (*living*). A PAST PARTICIPLE usually adds *-d* or *-ed* to the dictionary form (*lived*), although irregular verbs form the past participle in other ways (*begun, swept*). A participle or PARTICIPIAL PHRASE usually serves as an adjective: *<u>Strolling</u> shoppers fill the malls.* A GERUND is the *-ing* form of a verb used as a noun. Gerunds and GERUND PHRASES can do whatever nouns can do: *<u>Shopping</u> satisfies personal needs.* An INFINITIVE is the verb's dictionary form plus *to: to live.* Infinitives and INFINITIVE PHRASES may serve as nouns

(*To design a mall is to create an artificial environment*), as adverbs (*Malls are designed to make shoppers feel safe*), or as adjectives (*The environment supports the impulse to shop*).

Note that a verbal *cannot* serve as the only verb in the predicate° of a sentence. For that, it requires a helping verb:° *Shoppers were strolling*.

verb forms Verbs have five distinctive forms. The PLAIN FORM is the dictionary form: *A few artists live in town today*. The -S FORM adds -*s* or -*es* to the plain form: *The artist lives in town today*. The PAST-TENSE FORM usually adds -*d* or -*ed* to the plain form: *Many artists lived in town before this year*. Some verbs' past-tense forms are irregular, such as *began, fell, swam, threw, wrote*. The PAST PARTICIPLE is usually the same as the past-tense form, although, again, some verbs' past participles are irregular (*begun, fallen, swum, thrown, written*). The PRESENT PARTICIPLE adds -*ing* to the plain form: *A few artists are living in town today*.

REGULAR VERBS are those that add -*d* or -*ed* to the plain form for the past-tense form and past participle. IRREGULAR VERBS create these forms in irregular ways (see above).

verb phrase See *phrase*. A verb° of more than one word that serves as the predicate° of a sentence: *The movie has started*.

voice The form of a verb° that tells whether the sentence subject° performs the action or is acted upon. In the ACTIVE VOICE the subject acts: *The city controls rents*. In the PASSIVE VOICE the subject is acted upon: *Rents are controlled by the city*. The actor in a passive sentence may be stated (*the city*) or not stated: *Rents are controlled*. See also pp. 26–27.

INDEX

A

a, an
  capitalization in titles, 87
  choosing between, 139
  rules for use of (ESL), 42–44
Abbreviations
  a vs. *an* with, 139
  acceptable, 90–92
  BC, AD, AM, PM, no., $,
    90–91
  for calendar designations, 91
  for courses of instruction, 92
  for frequently used terms, 90
  for geographical names, 91
  Latin, 91
  for names of people, 91
  period in, 52, 90
  with specific dates and num-
    bers, 90–91
  in technical writing, 90, 91–92
  for titles with names, 90
  for units of measurement, 90
Absolute phrases, 55, 151
Abstract, dissertation, MLA
  style for, 113
Abstract words, 12–13
accept, except, 139
Acknowledgment of sources
  necessity for, 99–100, 103
  style guides for, 103–04
  using APA style, 125–34
  using CBE style, 134–38
  using *Chicago Manual* style,
    118–25
  using MLA style, 104–18
Active voice
  consistency in use of, 26
  definition of, 26, 151
  vs. passive voice, 16, 26–27
AD, BC, 90–91
Address, direct, 154
Address (lecture)
  MLA style for, 118
  underlining (italics) for,
    88–89

Addresses (street, city, state),
  comma with, 56
  numerals for, 93
Adjectives
  vs. adverbs, 40
  comma with two or more, 56
  comparative and superlative
    forms of, 40–41
  definition of, 40, 151
  hyphen in compound, 85
  irregular, 41
  after linking verbs, 40
  to modify nouns and pro-
    nouns, 40
  order of (ESL), 45–46
  present vs. past participles as
    (ESL), 42
  proper, capitalization of,
    86–87
Adverbs, 40–44. *See also*
    Conjunctive adverbs
  vs. adjectives, 40
  comparative and superlative
    forms of, 40–44
  definition of, 40–44, 151
  irregular, 41
  to modify verbs, adjectives,
    adverbs, 40–44
  semicolon with main clauses
    related by, 55
  in two-word verbs (ESL),
    31–32
advice, advise, 139
affect, effect, 139
after, 161
Afterword of book, MLA style
  for, 112
Agreement, definition of, 151
Agreement of pronouns and
    antecedents, 35–37
  with antecedents joined by
    and, 36
  with antecedents joined by
    or or *nor*, 36
  definition of, 35–36

Agreement of pronouns and antecedents (*continued*)
with *everyone* and other indefinite pronouns, 33–37
with *team* and other collective nouns, 37
Agreement of subjects and verbs, 27–30
definition of, 27
with *everyone* and other indefinite pronouns, 28
with intervening words, 27–28
with inverted word order, 29–30
with linking verbs, 30
with singular words ending in -*s*, 29
with subjects joined by *and*, 28
with subjects joined by *or* or *nor*, 28
with *team* and other collective nouns, 29
with *who, which,* or *that*, 29
Aircraft names, underlining (italics) for, 89
all, 28, 155
all ready, already, 139
all right, 139
all together, altogether, 140
allusion, illusion, 140
Almanac, MLA style for, 112
a lot, 140
although, 161
AM, PM, 90–91
American Psychological Association style. *See* APA style
among, between, 140
amount, number, 140
an, a. See *a, an*
and, 153
antecedents joined by, 36
comma with, 53
and coordination, 2–3
for correcting comma splices or fused sentences, 49
parallelism with, 4–5
subjects joined by, 28
vs. &, 91
and/or, 140

Anonymous work
APA style for: in parenthetical citation, 127; in reference list, 130, 132
CBE style for, 137
Chicago Manual style for, 122
MLA style for: in list of works cited, 111; in parenthetical citation, 106
Antecedents
agreement of pronouns and, 35–37
definition of, 37, 151
reference of pronouns to, 37–39
Anthology
APA style for, 131–32
Chicago Manual style for, 123
MLA style for, 112
anxious, eager, 140
any, 28, 155
anybody, 155
anybody, any body; anyone, any one, 140
any more, anymore, 140
anyone, 155
anything, 155
anyways, anywheres, 140
APA style
for document format, 79–80
for electronic sources, 133–34
for long quotations, 64
notes with, 127–28
for parenthetical citations, 125–27
for reference list, 128–34
Apostrophe, 60–62
to form contractions, 61
to form plurals of letters, etc., used as words, 62
to form possessives, 60–61
misuses of, 61
Appalachian English, 9
Appositive
comma with, 54–55
definition of, 54, 151
form of pronoun in, 34–35
are, is, 140
Articles (*a, an, the*)
capitalization in titles, 87
choosing between *a* and *an*, 139

definition of, 151
rules for use of (ESL), 42–44
Articles in periodicals
APA style for, 131–32
CBE style for, 137–38
Chicago Manual style for, 123
MLA style for, 112–13, 114, 116
titles of, quotation marks for, 64–65
Art works
Chicago Manual style for, 124
MLA style for, 117
underlining (italics) for titles of, 88–89
as, 159, 161
form of pronouns after, 35
misuses of, 141–42
as, like, 145
as if, 161
as long as, 161
Associations, capitalization of names of, 86–87
as though, 161
at this point in time, 141
Audience. *See* "Writer's Checklist" *inside front cover*
Authors
APA style for: in parenthetical citations, 125–27; in reference list, 128–33
CBE style for, 136–38
Chicago Manual style for, 120–23
MLA style for: in list of works cited, 107–18; in parenthetical citations, 104–07
Auxiliary verbs. *See* Helping verbs
awful, awfully, 141
a while, awhile, 141

B
bad, badly, 40, 141
BC, AD, 90–91
BCE, CE, 90–91
be
forms of (ESL), 19–20
as helping verb, 19–20
as linking verb, 30, 156
in subjunctive mood, 25–26

because, 161
before, 159, 161
being as, being that, 141
beside, besides, 141
between, among, 115
Biased language, 10–11
Bible
capitalization of, 87
colon for citations of, 60
no underlining (italics) for, 89
Bibliography
APA style for, 125–34
CBE style for, 134–38
Chicago Manual style for, 118–25
MLA style for, 107–18
style guides for, 103–04
Black English, 9
Boldface, for emphasis, 72
Books
APA style for, 130–31
CBE style for, 136–37
Chicago Manual style for, 121–23
MLA style for, 109–12, 115
subdivisions of, quotation marks for, 64
titles of: capitalization in, 88–89; underlining (italics) for, 88–89
both . . . and, 5, 153
Brackets
with equations, 69
with quotations, 69
bring, take, 141
Business letters, format for, 81–83
but, 153
comma with, 53
and coordination, 2
for correcting comma splices or fused sentences, 49
parallelism with, 4–5

C
can, may, 141
Capitalization, 86–88
of *a, an, the* in titles, 87
in APA style, 129
in CBE style, 136
of days, months, holidays, 86

Capitalization (*continued*)
in direct quotations, 98
in electronic mail, 83
of first word in sentence, 86
of government agencies, 86
of historical events, documents, periods, movements, 86
of languages, 87
in MLA style, 108
of organizations and associations, 86–87
of persons and places, 86
of proper nouns and adjectives, 86–87
of races and nationalities, 87
of religions and religious terms, 87
of science terms, 86
of titles of persons, 88
of titles of works, 87
Case of pronouns, 33–35
in appositive, 34–35
in compound subject or object, 33
definition of, 33, 152
before gerund, 35
with infinitive, 35
as subject complement, 33
after *than* or *as*, 35
we vs. *us* with noun, 34–35
who vs. *whom*, 33–34
CBE style
for document format, 80–81
for electronic sources, 138
for long quotations, 64
for numbered reference list, 135–38
for numbered text citations, 134–35
CD-ROM sources
APA style for, 133
Chicago Manual style for, 124
MLA style for, 114
CE, BCE, 90–91
Central idea. *See* "Writer's Checklist" *inside front cover*
Charts, in documents, 75–76
Chicago Manual style
for document format, 78
for electronic sources, 124–25

for endnotes or footnotes, 118–25
for list of works cited, 118–25
for long quotations, 63–64
Citations. *See* APA style; CBE style; *Chicago Manual* style; MLA style
Clause(s)
comma with, 48–50, 53
conciseness of, 15
conjunctive adverbs with, 50, 58
coordinating conjuctions with, 49, 53
definition of, 152
main, 127. *See also* Main clause(s)
semicolon with, 49, 50, 57–58
subordinate, 127. *See also* Subordinate clause(s)
Clichés, 13
climatic, climactic, 141
Collection. *See* Anthology
Collective noun
and agreement of pronoun, 37
and agreement of verb, 29
definition of, 152
Colloquial language, 8–9
Colon, 59–60
vs. dash, 66
misuse of, 59
with quotation marks, 65
uses of, 59–60, 65
Comma, 53–57
with absolute phrases, 55
between adjectives, 56
with conjunctive adverbs and transitional expressions such as *however* and *for example*, 50, 58
with coordinating conjunctions such as *and* or *but*, 53
coordination with, 2
vs. dash, 66
in dates, addresses, place names, numbers, 56
with direct address, 55
with identifying words for quotations, 57

with introductory elements, 53–54

between items in series, 55–56

with main clauses joined by *and, but*, etc., 53

misuses of, 53–56

with nonrestrictive elements, 54–55, 157

with parenthetical expressions, 55

with phrases of contrast, 55

with quotations, 57, 65

splices, 48–50

with *yes* and *no*, 55

Commands, 47, 52

Comma splices, 48–50, 152

Common knowledge, 99

Comparative form, 152

Comparison, 40–41, 152

complement, compliment, 142

Complement, subject, 33, 161

Complex sentence, 160

Compound adjectives, hyphen in, 85

Compound-complex sentence, 160

Compound constructions
comma in, 53
for coordination, 2–3
definition of, 152
parallelism with, 4–5
semicolon in, 57–58

Compound numbers, hyphen in, 85

Compound objects, objective pronoun case for, 33

Compound sentence, 160

Compound subjects
agreement of verbs with, 28
subjective pronoun case for, 33

Compound words, 61, 85

Computerized sources
APA style for, 133–34
CBE style for, 138
Chicago Manual style for, 124–25
MLA style for, 107, 114–16

Conciseness, achieving, 13–16
combining sentences, 16

cutting empty words and phrases, 14

cutting repetition, 15

eliminating expletives (*there is, it is*), 16

focusing on subject and verb, 14

reducing clauses and phrases, 16

using active voice, 16

using strong verbs, 15

Concrete words, 12–13

Conditional sentence or statement
definition of, 153
and mood of verb, 25–26
and tense sequence, 23–24

Conjunctions. *See also* Coordinating conjunctions; Correlative conjunctions; Subordinating conjunctions
capitalization in titles, 87
definition of , 153

Conjunctive adverbs
and comma splices, 50
comma with, 50
definition of, 153
list of, 153
semicolon with main clauses related by, 57–58

Connotation, 12

conscience, conscious, 142

Consistency
of pronouns, 39
of verb mood, 25
of verb tense, 22
of verb voice, 26

continual, continuous, 142

Contractions, 61, 153

Coordinating conjunctions
comma with, 53
coordination with, 2–3
for correcting comma splices or fused sentences, 49
definition of, 153
list of, 153
parallelism with, 4–5

Coordination, 2–3
definition of, 153
excessive, 3
parallelism with, 4–5

Coordination (*continued*)
  punctuation with, 53
Corporate author
  APA style for: in parentheti-
    cal citation, 126; in refer-
    ence list, 130
  MLA style for: in list of works
    cited, 111; in parenthetical
    citation, 106
Corrections, in documents, 73
Correlative conjunctions
  definition of, 153
  list of, 153
  parallelism with, 5
could of. See have, of
Council of Biology Editors
    style. *See* CBE style
Count nouns
  and *a/an, the* (ESL), 42–43
  definition of, 153
Courses of instruction, abbre-
    viation of, 90
Creole, 9
criteria, 142

D
-d. See -ed, -d
Dangling modifiers, 46, 153
Dashes, 66–67
  colon vs., 67
  comma vs., 66
  forming and spacing, in doc-
    ument, 66, 72
  hyphen vs., 66
  with quotation marks, 65
  uses of, 66
data, 142
Databases, electronic
  APA style for, 133
  CBE style for, 138
  Chicago Manual style for,
    124–25
  MLA style for, 114–16
Dates
  BC (*BCE*) and *AD* (*CE*) with,
    90–91
  commas in, 56
  numerals vs. words for, 92
Days of week
  abbreviation of, 91
  capitalization of, 86
Decimals, numerals for, 93

Defined terms, 65, 89
Dependent clause. *See*
    Subordinate clause(s)
Details, 7, 13
Determiner, 154
device, devise, 142
Dialect
  definition of, 9
  uses of, 9
Dialog, format of, 64
Diction
  appropriate, 8–11
  conciseness and, 13–16
  exact, 11–13
different from, different than,
    142
Direct address, 55, 154
Direct object, 154
Direct questions, 52, 154
Direct quotations. *See* Quota-
    tions, direct
Discussion list, MLA style for,
    115
disinterested, uninterested, 142
Diskette sources
  APA style for, 133
  CBE style for, 138
  Chicago Manual style for, 124
  MLA style for, 114
Dissertation abstract, MLA
    style for, 113
Documentation of sources. *See
    also* Plagiarism
  APA style for, 125–34
  CBE style for, 134–38
  Chicago Manual style for,
    118–25
  definition of, 103
  MLA style for, 104–18
  necessity for, 99
  style guides for, 103–04
  in writing process. *See*
    "Writer's Checklist" *inside
    front cover*
Documents, format for, 71–84
  for academic papers, 77–81
  for business (job-applica-
    tion) letters, 81–83
  headings, 73–74
  lists, 74
  margins, 73
  paper, 71

print quality, 71
punctuation for, 72
for résumés, 83, 84
tables and illustrations in,
74–77
text, 71–72
type, 71–72
underlining in, 72
white space, 72–74
don't, doesn't, 142
Double comparisons, 41
Double negatives, 41–42, 154
Double talk or doublespeak,
10
Draft. *See* "Writer's Checklist"
inside front cover
due to, 142

E
each, 28, 36, 155
eager, anxious, 140
-ed, -d, as verb endings, 18–19
Editing. *See* "Writer's Check-
list" *inside front cover*
Edition, later
APA style for, 131
Chicago Manual style for, 122
MLA style for, 111
Editorial, MLA style for, 113
Editors
APA style for, 130
CBE style for, 136–37
Chicago Manual style for, 122
MLA style for, 110–11
effect, affect, 139
e.g., 91
either, 155
either . . . or, 5, 153
Electronic mail
citation of: APA style for,
133; MLA style for, 114
format for, 83
Electronic sources
APA style for, 133–34
CBE style for, 138
Chicago Manual style for,
124–25
MLA style for: in list of works
cited, 114–16; in paren-
thetical citations, 107
elicit, illicit, 143
Ellipsis mark, 67–68, 154

Emphasis
boldface for, 72
exclamation point for, 52
subordination for, 3–4
underlining (italics) for, 72,
89
Endnotes. *See* Notes
End punctuation marks, 52
English as a second language
(ESL)
adjective order, 45–46
helping verbs and main
verbs, 19–20
omitted subject or verb, 47
participles as adjectives,
42–44
use of articles, 42–44
verb plus gerund or infinitive, 30–31
verb plus particle, 31–32
verb tense sequence, 22–25
enthused, 143
Envelope for job-application
letter, 83
ESL. *See* English as a second
language
Essays, quotation marks for
titles of, 64–65
-es. See -s, -es
et al., 91, 105, 110, 126
etc., 91, 143
Euphemisms, 10
Evaluation of research sources,
95–96
even if, 161
even though, 161
every, 28, 36
everybody, 155
everybody, every body, 143
everyday, every day, 143
everyone, 28, 155
everything, 155
everywheres, 143
except, accept, 139
Exclamation point, 52, 65–66
Expletive constructions, 16, 29,
154
explicit, implicit, 143

F
farther, further, 143
feel, 40, 143

fewer, less, 143
Films
  APA style for, 133
  MLA style for, 117
  title of, underlining (italics)
    for, 89
First draft. *See* "Writer's Check-
    list" *inside front cover*
First person, 158
Footnotes. *See* Notes
for
  with comma, 53
  as coordinating conjunction,
    2–3, 53, 153
  as preposition, 159
Foreign words, underlining
    (italics) for, 89
Foreword to book, MLA style
    for, 112
Formatting documents. *See*
    Documents, format for
Fractions
  hyphens with, 85
  numerals for, 93
Fragment. *See* Sentence frag-
    ment
FTP (File Transfer Protocol)
    site source
  MLA style for, 115–16
  APA style for, 134
Fused sentences, 48–49, 154
Future perfect progressive
    tense, 163
Future perfect tense, 154, 163
Future progressive tense, 162
Future tense, 154, 162

G
Gender, 154
General vs. specific words,
    12–13
Generic *he*, 37. *See also* Sexist
    language
Geographical names
  abbreviation of, 91
  capitalization of, 87
  commas with, 56
Gerunds and gerund phrases
  definition of, 130, 163
  following verb (ESL), 30–31
  possessive before, 35

get, 144
good, well, 144
Government agencies, capital-
    ization of, 86
Government document
  APA style for, 133
  CBE style for, 138
  Chicago Manual style for,
    124
  MLA style for: in list of
    works cited, 116–17; in
    parenthetical citation, 106
Graphs, in documents, 75–76

H
hanged, hung, 144
have, of, 144
he, 158
  case forms of, 152
  and sexist language, 11, 37,
    144
he, she; he/she, 144
Headings, in documents, 73,
    80
Helping verbs (auxiliary verbs),
    19–20, 155
herself/himself, 146
hisself, 144
Historical events and periods,
    capitalization of, 86
Holidays
  abbreviation of, 86
  capitalization of, 91
Homonyms, 12
hopefully, 144
however, 50, 58, 153
hung, hanged, 144
Hyphen
  to attach prefixes and suf-
    fixes, 85
  with capitalized words, 85
  in compound adjectives,
    85
  vs. dash, 66
  in fractions and compound
    numbers, 85
  use in forming dash, 66, 72
  in word division, 85

I
I, case forms of, 152

Idioms
  definition of, 155
  with prepositions, 13
  with verbs (ESL), 30
i.e., 91
if, 161
if, whether, 144
if only, 161
illicit, elicit, 143
illusion, allusion, 140
Illustrations, in documents,
    74–77
Imperative mood, 156
implicit, explicit, 143
imply, infer, 145
Indefinite pronouns
  alternative to *he* with, 37
  definition of, 155
  list of, 155
  pronoun agreement with,
    36–37
  verb agreement with, 28
Independent clause. *See* Main
    clause(s)
Indicative mood, 156
Indirect object, 155
Indirect quotation
  definition of, 155
  no quotation marks with,
    62
  and sequence of verb tenses
    (ESL), 24–25
Indirect source
  APA citation for, 127
  MLA citation for, 90
infer, imply, 145
Infinitives and infinitive
    phrases
  definition of, 155, 163–64
  following verb (ESL), 30–31
  objective case with, 35
  split, 45
Information service, APA style
    for, 132
-ing
  in gerund, 155, 163
  in present participle, 163
  in progressive tenses, 19–20,
    160, 162–63
in order that, 161
Interjections, 156

Interview
  APA style for, 133
  MLA style for, 118
Intransitive verb, 156
Introducing borrowed material
    (quotations, summaries,
    paraphrases), 101–02
Introduction to book, MLA
    style for, 112
Introductory element, comma
    with, 53–54
Inverted word order, subject-
    verb agreement and, 29–30
irregardless, 145
Irregular verbs, 18, 163
is, are, 140
is when, is where, 145
it, 158
  case forms of, 152
  possessive of, 61
  vague reference of, 38
Italics. *See* Underlining (italics)
it is, 16
its, it's, 145

J
Job-application letters, 81–83
Journals (periodicals)
  APA style for, 131–32,
    133–34
  CBE style for, 137–38
  Chicago Manual style for,
    123, 124–25
  MLA style for, 112–13, 114,
    116

K
kind of, sort of, type of, 145

L
Language. *See* Words
Languages, capitalization of
    names of, 87
Latin abbreviations, 91
lay, lie, 145
Lecture, MLA style for, 118
less, fewer, 143
Letters (correspondence)
  business (job application),
    81–83
  MLA style for, 117–18

Letters (of alphabet)
apostrophe for omission of,
61
forming plurals of, 62
underlining (italics) for, 89
Letter to the editor, MLA style
for, 113
lie, lay, 145
like, as, 145
Limiting modifiers, 45
Linking verbs
adjectives vs. adverbs after,
40
agreement with subjects, 30
definition of, 156
list of, 156
List of works cited. *See* APA
style; CBE style; *Chicago
Manual* style; MLA style
Lists, in documents, 74
literally, 145–46
Literary works, MLA citations
for, 106
Long quotations, set off from
text, 63–64
loose, lose, 146

M
Magazines
APA style for, 132
CBE style for, 138
Chicago Manual style for,
123
MLA style for, 112–13, 114,
116
Magnetic tape source, MLA
style for, 114
Main clause(s)
comma splice with, 49–51
conjunctive adverb and
semicolon to connect, 50,
57–58
coordination of, 2–3
definition of, 156
fused, 49–51
joined by comma and coor-
dinating conjunction, 53
semicolon to connect, 57
vs. subordinate clause, 152
Main verb, 19–20, 21, 156
Manuscripts, format for. *See*
Documents, format for

Margins, in documents, 73
Mass nouns. *See* Noncount
nouns
may, can, 141
may be, maybe, 146
may of. See have, of
Meanings of words, 12
Measurement, abbreviations of
units of, 91
media, 121
might of. See have, of
Misplaced modifiers, 44–46,
156
MLA style, 104–18
for document format,
77–78
for electronic sources, 107,
114–16
for list of works cited,
107–18
for long quotations, 63
notes with, 107
for parenthetical citations,
104–07
Modals, 21. *See also* Helping
verbs
Modern Language Association
style. *See* MLA style
Modifiers, 40–44
adjectives and adverbs,
40–44
conciseness of, 15
dangling, 46, 153
definition of, 156
irregular, 41
misplaced, 44–46
present vs. past participles as
(ESL), 42
verb forms as, 17, 163–64
Money amounts
abbreviations of, 91
numerals for, 93
Months of year
abbreviation of, 91
capitalization of, 86
MOO, MUD, MLA style for,
116
Mood of verbs, 25–26, 156
Movie. *See* Film
Ms., 81
Multiple authors
APA style for: in parentheti-

cal citation, 126–27; in reference list, 130
CBE style for, 136–38
Chicago Manual style for, 121–22
MLA style for: in list of works cited, 110; in parenthetical citation, 105
Multivolume book
APA style for, 131
Chicago Manual style for, 122
MLA style for: in list of works cited, 111; in parenthetical citation, 105
Musical composition
MLA style for, 117
title of: quotation marks for song, 64; underlining (italics) for long work, 88
must of. See have, of
myself, 146

N
Names of persons
abbreviation of, 91
capitalization of, 86
titles with, 90
Nationalities, capitalization of, 87
NB, 91
neither, 155
neither . . . nor, 153
Newsgroup, MLA style for, 115
Newspapers
APA style for, 132
CBE style for, 138
Chicago Manual style for, 123
MLA style for, 113, 114, 116
no, comma with, 55
nobody, 155
Noncount nouns
and *a/an, the*, 43–44
definition of, 157
none, 28, 155
Nonprint sources
APA style for, 133–34
CBE style for, 138
Chicago Manual style for, 124–25

MLA style for, 114–18
Nonrestrictive elements, 54, 157
Nonstandard language. *See* Dialect
no one, 28, 155
nor
and agreement of pronoun, 36
and agreement of verb, 28
not . . . but, 153
Notes
Chicago Manual style for: footnotes vs. endnotes in, 119; format of, 118–25; models of, 121–25
with parenthetical citations: APA style for, 127–28; MLA style for, 107
Note taking, 96–98
nothing, 155
not only . . . but also, 5, 153
Nouns
apostrophes with possessive, 60–61
capitalization of, 86–87
cases of, 34
collective, 29
count, 42–43
definition of, 157
noncount, 43–44
plurals of, 43–44
proper, 44, 86–87
nowheres, 121
now that, 161
Number
definition of, 157
pronoun-antecedent agreement in, 35–37
subject-verb agreement in, 27–30
number, amount, 140
Numbers, 92–93
abbreviations with, 92
in academic and business writing, 92
apostrophe to form plurals of, 61
at beginnings of sentences, 93
commas in, 56
hyphen in, 85
numerals vs. words for, 92
underlining (italics) for, 89

O
Object
    compound, 33
    definition of, 157
    direct, 154
    indirect, 155
    of infinitive, 35
    objective case for, 33–34
    of preposition, 157
    of verb, 157
Objective case, 33–34, 152, 157
of, *have*, 144
OK, O.K., okay, 121
once, 161
one, 155
Online posting, MLA style for, 115
Online sources
    APA style for, 133–34
    CBE style for, 138
    Chicago Manual style for, 124–25
    MLA style for, 114–16
or, 153
    and agreement of pronoun, 36
    and agreement of verb, 28
Organization names, capitalization of, 86–87

P
Pamphlets, underlining (italics) for titles of, 88
Paper, used for documents, 71
Paragraphs in documents, 73. *See also* "Writer's Checklist" *inside front cover*
Parallelism, 4–5, 157
Paraphrase
    avoiding plagiarism with, 99–100
    definition of, 97–98
    documenting, 100, 103–38
    introducing, in a paper, 101–02
    vs. summary and direct quotation, 96–97
Parentheses
    with other punctuation, 67
    uses of, 67

Parenthetical citations
    APA style, 125–27
    MLA style, 104–07
Parenthetical expressions
    commas for, 55
    definition of, 55, 67, 157
    parentheses for, 67
Participial phrase, 163
Participles and participial phrases, 138. *See also* Past participle; Present participle
Particle
    definition of, 31, 158
    in two-word verbs (ESL), 31–32
Parts of speech, 158
Passive voice
    vs. active voice, 16, 26–27, 164
    avoiding, 16, 26–27
    definition of, 26, 158
    formation of, 20
    uses of, 26–27
Past participle
    be forms with (ESL), 20
    definition of, 158, 163
    have forms with (ESL), 20
    irregular, 18, 163, 164
    vs. present participle (ESL), 42
Past perfect progressive tense, 162
Past perfect tense, 23, 162
Past progressive tense, 162
Past tense, 18, 23, 162, 163, 164
Past-tense form, 164
people, persons, 121
percent (per cent), percentage, 147
Percentages, 93
Perfect tenses, 22, 23, 159, 162–63
Performance
    APA style for, 133
    MLA style for, 117
Period
    with abbreviations, 52, 90
    correcting comma splice or fused sentence with, 49
    with quotation marks, 65

space with, in document, 72
uses of, 52, 90
Periodicals. S*ee also* Articles in
  periodicals
  APA style for, 131–32,
    133–34
  CBE style for, 137–38
  Chicago Manual style for,
    123, 124–25
  MLA style for, 112–13, 114,
    116
  underlining (italics) for titles
    of, 88
Person
  definition of, 158
  pronoun-antecedent agree-
    ment in, 35–37
  shifts in, 39
  subject-verb agreement in,
    27–30
Personal online site, MLA style
  for, 115
Personal pronouns
  agreement with antecedents,
    37–39
  case forms of, 33, 152
  definition of, 158
  list of, 158
  no apostrophe with posses-
    sives of, 61
persons, *people*, 121
phenomena, 146
Phrase(s)
  absolute, 55, 151
  definition of, 158
  gerund, 163
  infinitive, 163
  participial, 163
  prepositional, 159
  subordination with, 3–4
  verb, 163
  verbal, 163
Place names
  abbreviation of, 91
  capitalization of, 86
  comma with, 56
Plagiarism, 98–100
  checklist for avoiding, 100
  citing sources to avoid,
    99–100
  common knowledge vs., 99

definition of, 98
independent material vs.,
  99
Plain form, of verbs, 18, 20–21,
  159
Play
  MLA style for: in list of works
    cited, 117; in parenthetical
    citation, 107
  title of, underlining (italics)
    for, 88
Plurals
  apostrophe with possessives
    of, 60–61
  articles with (ESL), 43–44
  definition of, 159
  of letters, numbers, and
    words named as words, 62
  misuse of apostrophe with, 61
plus, 147
PM, *AM*, 90–91
Poetry
  format of quotations from,
    63–64, 68
  slash between lines of, 69
  titles of: quotation marks
    for short, 64–65; underlin-
    ing (italics) for long, 88
Point size, for text in documents, 72
Positive form, 152
Possessive case
  apostrophe with, 60–61
  definition of, 152, 159
  and noun or pronoun form,
    33
precede, *proceed*, 147
Predicate, 159
Preface to book, MLA style for,
  112
Prefixes, hyphen to attach, 85
prejudice, *prejudiced*, 147
Prepositional phrase, 159
Prepositions
  capitalization in titles, 87
  definition of, 159
  in idioms, 13
  list of, 159
  objects of, 159
  in two-word verbs (ESL),
    31–32

Present participle
definition of, 159, 164
forms of *be* with (ESL), 19–20
vs. past participle (ESL), 42
Present perfect progressive tense, 162
Present perfect tense, 22, 162
Present progressive tense, 162
Present tense, 21–22, 159, 162
Pretentious writing, 10
principal, principle, 147
Principal parts of verbs, 159
proceed, precede, 147
Professional online site, MLA style for, 115
Progressive tenses
definition of, 160, 162–63
formation of, 19 (ESL), 162–63
Pronouns, 33–39
agreement of, with antecedent, 35–37
case forms of, 33–35, 152
consistency of, 39
definition of, 160
everybody and other indefinite, 155
I, you, she, and other personal, 160
misuse of apostrophe with possessive, 61
reference of, to antecedent, 37–39
who, which, that, and other relative, 160
Proper nouns
articles with (ESL), 44
capitalization of, 86–87
definition of, 44, 86, 160
Prose, format of quotations from, 62–64
Punctuation, 52–69. *See also specific punctuation marks*
of absolute phrases, 55
with *and, but*, and other coordinating conjunctions, 53
of concluding elements, 54
at ends of sentences, 50
with *for example* and other transitional expressions, 50, 58
forming and spacing, in document, 72
with *however* and other conjunctive adverbs, 50, 58
of interrupting elements, 54–55
of introductory elements, 53–54
of linked main clauses, 53, 57
of nonessential elements, 54–55, 66, 67, 157
of nonrestrictive elements, 54, 157
of parenthetical expressions, 55, 69
of phrases of contrast, 55
of possessive case, 60–61
of quotations, 57, 62–64, 67–69
of restrictive elements, 54–55, 160
of series, 55–56, 58–59, 66–67
space with, in manuscript, 72
of titles of works, 60, 64
of words of direct address, 55
Purpose of essay. *See* "Writer's Checklist" *inside front cover*

Q
Question mark
with direct questions, 52
with quotation marks, 65–66
Questions
direct, 52, 154
indirect, 155
tag, 162
who vs. *whom* in, 33–34
Quotation marks, 62–65
for dialog, 64
for direct quotations, 62–64
with other punctuation, 65–66
for quotation within quotation, 62–63
single, 62–63
in source citations: APA style, 129; CBE style, 136; *Chicago Manual* style, 120; MLA style, 108
for titles of works, 64–65
for words being defined, 65

Quotations, direct
accuracy of, 97–98
avoiding plagiarism with, 100
brackets in, 69
changes in, 67–69
comma with, 57, 65
copying, 98
criteria for using, 97–98
definition of, 62, 154
of dialog, 64
displayed separately from
text, 63–64
documentation of, 103–38
ellipsis mark in, 67–68
introducing, in a paper,
101–02
long, set off from text, 63–64,
72
omissions from, 67–68
vs. paraphrase and sum-
mary, 96–98
of poetry, 63–64, 68
of prose, 62–64
punctuating identifying
words with, 57
quotation marks with, 62–
64
within quotations, 62–63
Quotations, indirect, 62, 155

R
Races of people, capitalization
of, 87
Radio programs. *See* Television
and radio programs
raise, rise, 147
rather than, 161
Readers. *See* "Writer's Checklist" *inside front cover*
real, really, 147
reason is because, 147
Recording
APA style for, 133
MLA style for, 117
title of: quotation marks
for song, 64; underlining
(italics) for long work, 88
Reference list. *See* APA style;
CBE style; *Chicago Manual*
style; MLA style
Reference of pronouns, 37–39
References. *See* APA style; CBE

style; *Chicago Manual*
style; MLA style
Regular verbs, 18, 164
Relative pronouns
case forms of, 33–34, 152
definition of, 160
list of, 160
and subject-verb agreement,
152
Religions and their followers,
capitalization of, 87
Repetition, unneeded, 15
Report, APA style for, 132
Research papers
APA documentation style,
125–34
avoiding plagiarism in,
99–100
CBE documentation style,
134–38
Chicago Manual documentation style, 118–25
citing sources in, 103–38
document format for, 71–81
evaluation of sources for,
95–96
introducing borrowed material in, 101–02
long quotations in, 63–64
MLA documentation style,
104–18
note taking for, 96–98
style guides for, 103
synthesis of sources for, 96
writing. *See* "Writer's Checklist" *inside front cover*
respectful, respective, 147
Restrictive elements
definition of, 54, 160
misuse of comma with,
54–55
Résumés, format for, 83, 84
Review
APA style for, 132
MLA style for, 113
Revision. *See* "Writer's Checklist" *inside front cover*
rise, raise, 147
Run-on sentence, 48–49

S
-*'s*, 60–61

-*s*, *-es*
  possessive of words ending
    in, 60–61
  verb agreement with nouns
    ending in, 29
  as verb ending, 18–19, 164
Scholarly project, MLA style
  for, 115
Second person, 158
Semicolon, 57–59
  with conjunctive adverbs
    such as *however* and tran-
    sitional expressions such
    as *for example*, 50, 58
  correcting comma splices or
    fused sentences with, 49,
    50
  misuse of, 57–59
  with quotation marks, 57, 65
  to separate main clauses,
    57–58
  in series, 57
sensual, sensuous, 147
Sentence(s)
  capitalization of first word
    in, 86
  complex, 160
  compound, 160
  compound-complex, 160
  conciseness of, 13–16
  definition of, 160
  fused, 48–49
  length of, 6–7
  number at beginning of, 93
  vs. sentence fragment, 47–48
  simple, 160
  variety in, 6–7
Sentence combining, for conciseness, 16
Sentence fragment, 47–48,
  160–61
  tests for, 47–48
Sequence of tenses, 23–25
Series
  colon to introduce, 59, 67
  comma with, 55–56
  dash with, 66–67
  definition of, 161
  semicolon with, 57
Series (publication), MLA style
  for, 112

set, sit, 147
Sexist language, 10–11, 37
she, case forms of, 152
she, he; *he/she*, 144
Shifts
  in pronouns, 39
  in verb mood, 25
  in verb tense, 22
  in verb voice, 26
Ship names, underlining
  (italics) for, 89
Short stories, quotation marks
  for titles of, 64–65
should of. See have, of
Simple future tense, 162
Simple past tense, 162
Simple present tense, 162
Simple sentence, 160
since, 147, 159, 161
sit, set, 147
Slang, 8
Slash, 69
so, 2, 4, 53, 153
Software
  APA style for, 133–34
  CBE style for, 138
  Chicago Manual style for,
    124–25
  MLA style for, 116
some, 155
somebody, 28, 155
somebody, some body; *someone, some one*, 148
someone, 155
something, 155
*sometime, sometimes, some
  time*, 148
somewheres, 148
Songs, quotation marks for
  titles of, 64–65
sort of, type of, kind of, 145
so that, 161
Source citations. *See* APA style;
  CBE style; *Chicago Manual*
  style; MLA style
Sources
  documentation of: APA
    style, 125–34; CBE style,
    134–38; *Chicago Manual*
    style, 118–25; MLA style,
    104–18

evaluation of, 95–96
notes from, 96–98
plagiarism vs. acknowledgment of, 98–100
synthesis of, 96
Specific vs. general words, 12–13
Speeches, published, underlining (italics) for titles of, 88
Spelling, checking. *See* "Writer's Checklist" *inside front cover*
Split infinitives, 45, 161
Squinting modifier, 161
Standard English, 8, 9
Subject, of paper. *See* "Writer's Checklist" *inside front cover*
Subject, of sentence
active vs. passive voice and, 26
agreement of verb with, 27–30
compound, 33
definition of, 161
omitted (ESL), 47
subjective case for, 33
Subject complement
definition of, 162
subjective case for, 33
Subjective case, 33–34, 152
Subjunctive mood, 25–26, 156
Subordinate clause(s)
definition of, 161
vs. main clause, 152
misuse of semicolon with, 57–58
as sentence fragment, 50
and sequence of verb tenses (ESL), 23
subordination with, 3–4
Subordinating conjunctions
definition of, 161
list of, 162
in subordinate clauses, 3, 48
Subordination
definition of, 162
to emphasize main ideas, 3–4
for variety, 6–7
Subtitles
capitalization of, 87
colon with, 60
Suffixes, hyphen to attach, 85

Summary
avoiding plagiarism with, 99–100
definition of, 96–97
documentation of, 103–38
introducing, in a paper, 101–02
vs. paraphrase and direct quotation, 96–98
Superlative form, 152
supposed to, used to, 148
sure and, sure to, 148
Synchronous communication, MLA style for, 116
Synonyms, 12
Synthesis of research sources, 96

T

Tables, in documents, 74–75
Tag questions, 162
take, bring, 141
Taking notes. *See* Note taking
Technical writing, 9, 86, 90, 91, 92
Television and radio programs
MLA style for, 117
titles of: quotation marks for episodes, 64–65; underlining (italics) for programs, 88
Tense(s), 21–25
consistency in, 22
definitions of, 162–63
list and forms of, 162–63
perfect, uses of, 22
present, uses of, 21–22
sequence of, 22–25
Text, in format of document, 71–72
than, 161
than, as, pronoun after, 35
than, then, 148
that, 29, 38, 148, 160, 161
that, which, 148
the. *See* Articles
their, there, they're, 149
theirselves, 149
then, than, 148
there, they're, their, 149
there is/are, 16, 29–30

they, 39, 152, 158
they're, *their*, *there*, 149
Third person, 158
this, vague reference of, 38–39
though, 161
thru, 149
thus, 58, 153
till, 161
Time
  AM or *PM* with, 91
  colon to punctuate, 60
  numerals vs. words for, 93
Titles of papers
  capitalization of, 87
  format of: APA style for, 79–80; CBE style for, 80–81; *Chicago Manual* style for, 78; MLA style for, 77
Titles of persons
  abbreviations for, 90
  in business (job-application) letters, 81–83
  capitalization of, 88
Titles of works
  articles in periodicals, 64–65
  books, 87, 88
  capitalization of, 87
  colon before subtitle in, 60
  essays, 64–65
  films, 89
  musical compositions: long, 88; song, 64–65
  pamphlets, 88
  periodicals, 88
  plays, 88
  poems: long, 88; short, 64–65
  quotation marks for, 64–65
  short stories, 64–65
  speeches, published, 88
  subdivision of books, 64–65
  television and radio: episodes, 64–65; programs, 88
  underlining (italics) for, 88–89
  visual art, 89
to, 30–31, 155
to, *too*, *two*, 149
Topic, of paper. *See* Subject, of paper.
toward, *towards*, 149

Train names, underlining (italics) for, 89
Transitional expressions
  list of, 163
  punctuation with, 50, 58
  uses of, 163
Transitive verb, 20, 163
Translations
  APA style for, 130
  MLA style for, 111
Trite expressions, 13
try and, *try to*, 149
Turabian, *A Manual for Writers of Term Papers, Theses, and Dissertations*, 63, 78, 118
type of, *kind of*, *sort of*, 145, 149

U
Underlining (italics), 88–89
  for definitions, 89
  in document, 72
  for foreign words, 89
  for names of vehicles, 90
  in source citations: APA style, 129; CBE style, 136; *Chicago Manual* style, 120; MLA style, 108
  for titles of works, 88–89
  underlining vs. italics, 72, 88
  for words, etc., named as words, 62, 89
uninterested, *disinterested*, 142
unique, 149
unless, 161
until, 161
us, vs. *we*, with noun, 34–35
used to, *supposed to*, 148

V
Variety in sentences, 6–7
Verb(s), 18–32
  agreement with subjects, 27–30
  conditional sentences and (ESL), 23–24
  definition of, 163
  forms of, 18–21, 164
  gerund vs. infinitive following (ESL), 30–31
  helping, 19–20, 155

with helping verbs (ESL),
19–20
indirect quotations and
(ESL), 24–25
intransitive, 156
for introducing borrowed
material, 102
irregular, 18, 164
linking, 30, 40, 156
main, 156
misuse of apostrophe with,
61
mood, 25–26, 156
object of, 157
omitted (ESL), 47
with particles (ESL), 31–32
plain form of, 159, 164
principal parts of, 159
regular, 18, 164
strong vs. weak, for conciseness, 15
tenses of, 21–25, 162–63
transitive, 163
two-word (ESL), 31–32
voice of, 16, 26–27, 164
Verbals and verbal phrases,
163–64
Verb phrase, 164
Videotapes
APA style for, 133
MLA style for, 117
Visual art. *See* Art works
Voice of verbs, 16, 26–27, 164
Volumes
numerals for, 93
in source citations: APA style
for, 131; *Chicago Manual*
style for, 122; MLA style
for, 105, 111

when, 161
whenever, 161
where, 161
whereas, 161
wherever, 161
whether, *weather*, 149
whether . . . or, 5, 153
which, 29, 38, 160
which, *that*, 149
which, *who*, 150
while, 161
White space, in documents, 72
who, 160
agreement of verb with, 29
reference of, 38
vs. *whom*, 33–34
whoever, 160
who's, *whose*, 150
Word division, hyphen for, 85
Wordiness, avoiding, 13–16
Words, 8–11
appropriate, 8–11
concise, 13–16
exact, 11–12
Words used as words
plurals of, 62
quotation marks for, 65
underlining (italics) for, 62,
89
Works cited. *See* APA style;
CBE style; *Chicago Manual*
style; MLA style
World Wide Web site
MLA style for, 115–16
APA style for, 134
would have, 150
would of. *See* have, of
Writing process. *See* "Writer's
Checklist" *inside front
cover*

Y
yes, comma with, 55
yet, 2, 4, 53, 153
you, 150, 152, 158
your, *you're*, 150
yourself, 146

wait for, wait on, 149
we, 158
case forms of, 152
vs. *us*, with a noun, 34–35
weak verbs, conciseness and,
15
weasel words, 10
weather, whether, 149
well, good, 144

Z
Zip codes, 56

EDITING SYMBOLS

Your readers may use some of these symbols to mark editing you should do. Page numbers refer you to relevant sections of thi handbook.

ab	Faulty abbreviation 90	⌃	Comma 53
ad	Misuse of adjective or adverb 40	;	Semicolon 57
agr	Error in agreement 27, 35	:	Colon 59
		⌄	Apostrophe 60
ap	Apostrophe needed or misused 60	" "	Quotation marks 62
appr	Inappropriate word 8	— ( ) ... [ ] /	Dash, parentheses, ellipsis mark, brackets, slash 66
awk	Awkward construction	**par, ¶**	Start new paragraph
cap	Use capital letter 86	**pass**	Ineffective passive voice 16, 26
case	Error in pronoun form 33		
cit	Missing source citation or error in form of citation 103–38	**pn agr**	Error in pronoun-antecedent agreement 3.
con	Be more concise 13	**ref**	Error in pronoun reference 37
coord	Coordination needed 2		
cs	Comma splice 48	**rep**	Unnecessary repetition 15
d	Ineffective diction (word choice) 8–16	**run-on**	Run-on (fused) sentence 48
det	Add details 7		
dm	Dangling modifier 46	**shift**	Inconsistency 22, 25, 26, 39
emph	Emphasis lacking 3		
exact	Inexact word 11	**sp**	Misspelled word
frag	Sentence fragment 47	**spec**	Be more specific 7, 12
fs	Fused sentence 48	**sub**	Subordination needed 3
gl/us	See Glossary of Usage 139	**t**	Error in verb tense 21
hyph	Error in use of hyphen 85	**t seq**	Error in tense sequence 22
inc	Incomplete construction		
ital	Italicize (underline) 88	**trans**	Transition needed 163
k	Awkward construction	**und**	Underline (italicize) 88
lc	Use lowercase letter 86	**var**	Vary sentence structure
mm	Misplaced modifier 44	**vb**	Error in verb form 18
mng	Meaning unclear	**vb agr**	Error in subject-verb agreement 27
ms	Error in manuscript form 71	**w**	Wordy 13
		ww	Wrong word 11
no cap	Unnecessary capital letter 86	**//**	Faulty parallelism 4
		#	Separate with a space
no ⌃	Comma not needed 53	◡	Close up space
no ¶	No new paragraph needed	⟍	Delete
num	Error in use of numbers 92	t⌒e⌒h	Transpose letters or words
p	Error in punctuation 52–69	**x**	Obvious error
		^	Something missing
? !	Period, question mark, exclamation point 52	**??**	Document illegible or meaning unclear